Young Architects 22
Value

T0284575

Young Architects 22
Value

Acknowledgments by
Paul Lewis
Foreword by
Anna Puigjaner
Introduction by
Anne Rieselbach

David Eskenazi
d.esk

**Garrett Ricciardi
and Julian Rose**
Formlessfinder

Leslie Lok and Sasa Zivkovic
HANNAH

Isaac Michan Daniel
Michan Architecture

**Ivi Diamantopoulou
and Jaffer Kolb**
New Affiliates

**Luis Beltrán del Río García
and Andrew Sosa Martínez**
Vrtical

The Architectural
League of New York

Co-published by
The Architectural League of New York
and ORO Editions

The Architectural League of New York
594 Broadway, Suite 607
New York, NY 10012
www.archleague.org

ORO Editions
Publishers of Architecture, Art, and Design
Gordon Goff: Publisher
www.oroeditions.com

To read interviews with each firm,
please visit archleague.org.

© 2023 The Architectural League
of New York

All rights reserved. No part of this book may
be reproduced, stored in a retrieval system,
or transmitted in any form or by any means,
including electronic, mechanical, photocopying
of microfilming, recording, or otherwise (except
that copying permitted by Sections 107 and
108 of the U.S. Copyright Law and except by
reviewers for the public press) without written
permission from the publisher.

You must not circulate this book in any other
binding or cover and you must impose this
same condition on any acquirer.

Every reasonable attempt has been made to
identify owners of copyright. Errors or omissions
will be corrected in subsequent editions.

Except when noted, all images courtesy of
the architects and designers.

Editor Anne Rieselbach
Managing Editor Rafi Lehmann
Consulting Editor Andrea Monfried
Cover Design Pentagram /
Jena Sher Graphic Design
Interior Layout Jena Sher Graphic Design
Project Manager Jake Anderson

This publication is supported, in part, by
public funds from the New York City
Department of Cultural Affairs in partnership
with the City Council.

We thank ORO Editions for their in-kind
support for this publication.

The 2020 League Prize program was also made
possible by Hunter Douglas Architectural,
Rachel Judlowe, Elizabeth Kubany, and Tischler
und Sohn.

10 9 8 7 6 5 4 3 2 1 First Edition

Color Separations and Printing:
ORO Group Inc.
Printed in China.

Library of Congress Control Number:
2022914072
ISBN 978-1-957183-11-4

AR+D Publishing makes a continuous effort
to minimize the overall carbon footprint
of its publications. As part of this goal, AR+D,
in association with Global ReLeaf, arranges
to plant trees to replace those used in the
manufacturing of the paper produced for
its books. Global ReLeaf is an international
campaign run by American Forests, one
of the world's oldest nonprofit conservation
organizations. Global ReLeaf is American
Forests' education and action program that
helps individuals, organizations, agencies,
and corporations improve the local and global
environment by planting and caring for trees.

Contents

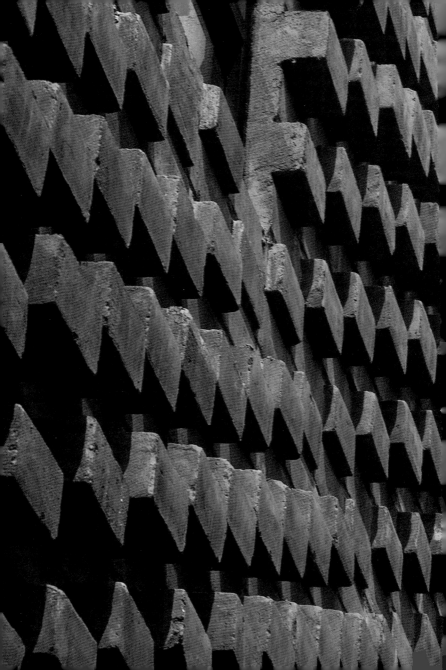

The Architectural League of New York
Board of Directors 2020–2021

President
Paul Lewis

Vice Presidents
Mario Gooden
Torkwase Dyson
Michael Bierut
Mary Margaret Jones
Nico Kienzl
Vishaan Chakrabarti
Tucker Viemeister
Kris Graves
Mabel O. Wilson

Secretary
Mary Burnham

Treasurer
Nat Oppenheimer

Directors
Amale Andraos
Stella Betts
Tatiana Bilbao
Fiona Cousins
Jared Della Valle
Leslie Gill
Frances Halsband
Steven Holl
Wendy Evans Joseph
Rachel Judlowe
Andy Klemmer
Joseph Mizzi
Gregg Pasquarelli
Thomas Phifer
Lyn Rice
Mark Robbins
Susan T. Rodriguez
Bradley Samuels
Annabelle Selldorf
Ken Smith
Karen Stein
Nader Tehrani
Calvin Tsao
Billie Tsien
Claire Weisz

Life Trustees
Walter Chatham
Barbara Jakobson
Suzanne Stephens
Robert A.M. Stern

Executive Director
Rosalie Genevro

Acknowledgments
Paul Lewis
President, The Architectural League of New York

Over the course of the 2020 League Prize for Young Architects + Designers—competition, exhibition, lectures, interviews, and now this book—the collective understanding of the year's theme, Value, grew to encompass a broader interpretation than the League Prize committee could possibly have expected. The converging crises of ecology and equity—not to mention the COVID-19 pandemic—required a reexamination of the agency and exercise of architecture, with considerations of value playing a pivotal role. The definition of value is ever changing, not fixed, and this publication marks specific creative responses within this evolving designation.

The influential and important League Prize, initiated in 1981, has consistently identified talented architects and designers whose work exemplifies inventive approaches to design, fabrication, and social engagement well before such approaches are implemented within the profession. The annual competition is open to all North American residents ten years or less out of an undergraduate or master's program. Entrants submit a design portfolio and text that addresses the competition theme, which is developed annually by a committee of recent winners. The new class of winners, profiled on the League's website, exhibit and discuss their work, bringing their ideas to an audience of peers and the broader design community.

Many thanks to the League Prize committee, Kutan Ayata, Mira Henry, and Kevin Hirth, for their thoughtful shaping of the competition theme and jury selection. It was a pleasure to serve on the jury with Lucia Allais, Anna Puigjaner, Nanako Umemoto, and the committee members. The very value of the League Prize is its continued quality, and we owe immense gratitude to Anne Rieselbach, the League's program director, and Catarina Flaksman, program manager, who not only guided the committee and the winners through this cycle but have sustained and advanced the program for years. The committee also worked with Michael Bierut and Britt Cobb of Pentagram, who once again translated the theme into a memorable graphic identity. Anne Carlisle, communications manager of the League, provided valuable counsel to the winners as they developed their digital installations on the League's website.

Rafi Lehmann, the League's current program manager, indefatigably served as managing editor for this publication, which again benefitted greatly from the enthusiasm and expertise of graphic designer Jena Sher and advisory editor Andrea Monfried. This book is a co-publication of The Architectural League and ORO Editions, and we extend our thanks to Gordon Goff and his team for their advocacy of the value of the printed medium.

The League Prize program was made possible by support from our financial supporters: Hunter Douglas Architectural; Rachel Judlowe; Elizabeth Kubany; Tischler und Sohn; and the Next Generation and J. Clawson Mills Funds of The Architectural League. The League Prize is also supported, in part, by public funds from the New York City Department of Cultural Affairs in partnership with the City Council.

Foreword
Anna Puigjaner
Juror; Cofounder, MAIO

The 2020 Architectural League Prize for Young Architects + Designers questioned how value operates in architecture, asking practitioners to reflect on this slippery term and its relationship to their work in a moment of historical transformation. Nowadays, the discipline is undergoing an enormous cultural redefinition that seeks to decolonize its nature. And in this shift, notions such as value have to be reconsidered in a way that requires architects and designers to take a position.

We must recall that ideas of value, worth, the good, the accepted carry with them shadowy counterparts: scorn, lack of worth, the bad, the unaccepted. The one is intrinsic to and undetachable from the other. We must also recall that architecture has not been neutral in constructing these forms of judgment and segregation.

In fact, maybe due to its own constitution, architecture has been since its origin a practice involved in the definition and perpetuation of values and behaviors that have established a deeply biased and unequal "normality." Most of these biased values are rooted within our culture; in architecture, they find, consciously or unconsciously, a form of expression and a tool for crystallization. These values are so built up by means of strong walls and steady roofs that those who benefit from them find it difficult to be aware of (or just don't want to be aware of) the imbalances created.

In the modern Western world, new forms of classification and biopolitical control were created based on an idea of objectivity that was generated through empirical modes of assessment. Under this regime, the family was defined and oversimplified as a heteropatriarchal structure, one that was increasingly related to a particular physical space, the house, which in turn became the architectural element that signified the family structure. Most of our built environment, and the way it is managed, owned, and used, has to do with this oversimplified relationship. Accompanying it was a set of social assumptions and requirements around the idea of housing, burdening the everyday life of those who do not align with those norms. People who do not fit into a family structure, who are nomadic, whose gender does not conform to binary divisions, whose bodies cannot perform as they are required to: anyone who cannot fit easily into modern formulations of efficiency and normality became excluded subaltern subjects.

Probably one of the most meaningful shifts that happened during the consolidation of this system of domestic order and control was the application of Taylorist and Fordist methods to housing design at the turn of the 20th century. This undertaking was not a naive reform: it coincided with the growing incorporation of women into industrial work, which demanded a reevaluation of care work. The kitchen became the symbol of a change in which the house turned into the space for caring and caring itself started to be treacherously presented as effortless. Thanks to efficient design, proper organization, and new domestic devices, care work could be performed "with ease." The Frankfurt kitchen, designed by Margarete Schütte-Lihotzky, became the icon of this gradually increasing technology; along with this process, care spaces became individualized, privatized, and reduced to the minimum allowance within which one body could perform.

The progressive seclusion and undervalue of care work through architecture has had an enormous impact on actual circumstances and likewise on the dependencies and imbalances generated. Even when such employment is paid and lawful, it is a type of work that is still extremely underrated and mostly performed by non-male and racialized bodies. The US Census Bureau data on the legal domestic workforce in New York City shows that 94 percent of this population is women, among them 38 percent Hispanic/Latinx, 27 percent Black (non-Hispanic/Latinx), and 18 percent Asian. And the median annual income is extremely low compared to that of all other workers, $21,320 versus $51,250.

Value, and how value is defined through architecture, has to be radically rethought in order to not perpetuate these systems of exclusion. We should not keep on building as we did; instead, we must undo, unlearn, unmake, unbuild the constructions that have excluded so many. Housing and its relationship to care work should be among the first architectural frameworks to be interrogated.

The question, then, is how to dismantle all of these structures. As Audre Lorde asserted in her famous lecture "The Master's Tools Will Never Dismantle the Master's House," we cannot replicate the formulas that created those imbalances but instead must find alternative ways of understanding the built environment. The 2020 League Prize winners share similar concerns and address various opportunities, though in different ways. The young firms remind us that we must stay outside our inherited ideological frame if we are to create a new one that will empower existing and new fields able to rethink the role of architecture within society.

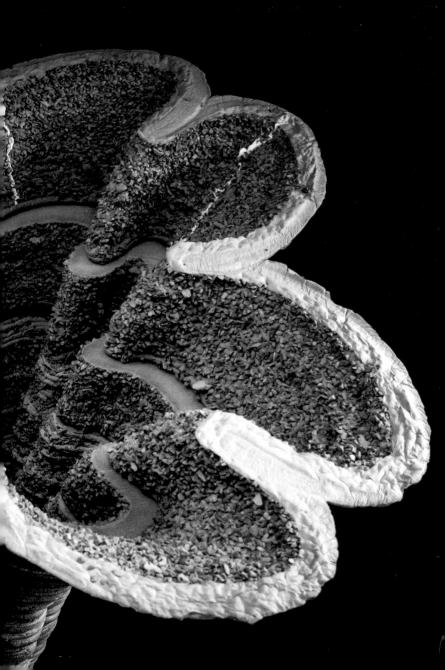

Introduction
Anne Rieselbach
Program Director, The Architectural League of New York

Value is a slippery construct in architecture, leading to thoughts of numbers, colors, measurement, worth, and ethics. Value can be personal or shared, analytical or sensorial. It suggests economic and aesthetic highs and lows and hints at the ideological urgencies that undergird and influence the production of architecture.

—Architectural League Prize 2020 Call for Entries

Value, the 2020 competition theme for the Architectural League Prize for Young Architects + Designers, asked entrants working "in a time of political and social precariousness" to demonstrate how "notions of value operate in [their] work" and to consider how value is manifested in the "processes of design and the forms of representation, and/or spaces of action." The portfolios submitted in response to this prompt explored a wide range of topics, among them sourcing and recycling materials; enlarging drawings or models to building scale; determining how, when, and why buildings should be constructed; and forming meaningful relationships with clients and communities.

Since the launch of the League Prize in 1981, winners have presented lectures and exhibited their work in New York City, often interpreting the annual theme though site-specific installations. But the pandemic forced a revision of both the lectures and the installations. Winners were tasked with transforming their proposals for physical exhibitions into online formats and encouraged to think outside conventional representational strategies. The revised plans took full advantage of the digital medium, using imagery, audio and video content, and interactive platforms to document work ranging from conceptual explorations to completed projects.

David Eskenazi, principal of d.esk, documented *Inhale, Exhale, Sag, Flex,* a scheme for flexible, easily installed public bathhouses on city-owned lots in Los Angeles. The primary function of this typology is to "clean and relax bodies that are worked out in the city" and also to allow "foreign bodies [to] care for themselves in a manner that is both personal and collective." Conceptual sketches, plans, sections, material studies, and models, as well as a video of paired paper pads undergoing iterative processes of dripping, ripping, and erasure, illustrate d.esk's proposal for a bifurcated building containing a steam house and a pool house. Both are dynamic: a quilt of water bladders enclosing the steam house fills as steam evaporates and bodies exhale, while removable building paper wraps the pool house. This dual system enables "both architecture and people [to] unrobe and collectively self-care," writes Eskenazi.

The Future of the Past, a video by Formlessfinder principals Garrett Ricciardi and Julian Rose, is at once travelogue and inquiry into the archaeological, industrial, and natural landscape of Kuwait. The video culminates in the firm's design for the Subbiyah Highway Archaeology and Infrastructure Research Center, which was commissioned for the 2020 Kuwait Pavilion at the Venice Architecture Biennale. A virtual passage through the landscape reveals the clashing priorities that have shaped the proposal: changing infrastructural needs, an active industrial landscape, and the desire to excavate, preserve, and display archaeological sites and artifacts. The designers write that reconciling these priorities "offer[s] a case study that could guide future development across the region and around the world."

HANNAH's *A Building Tale: The Story of Two Constructions, One Old Robot, and Bountiful Emerald Bugs* provides an interactive story about the making of the *Ashen Cabin*. Partners Leslie Lok and Sasa Zivkovic describe how the cabin, with its corbelled 3D-printed concrete structure and "undulating ash wood envelope," was built by means of "robotic routines and herculean manual labor." The designers present project documentation including photos, drone videos, and gifs; detailed written descriptions; and subjective impressions composed by peers, the construction team, collaborators, and cabin guests. Visitors selected texts and images on the installation site to experience "contemplations on the nature of construction, the fluffiness of spray foam, the ominous hum of an old robot, site making, wood bacon, ornamental concrete sausages, forest creatures, and the disastrous reign of the tiny Emerald Ash Borer."

In an early, pre-Covid scheme for a gallery installation, Isaac Michan Daniel, principal of Michan Architecture, planned a series of abstract carved models, each suggesting an adaptable design strategy rather than a specific building or building element. When the exhibition moved online, he decided instead to fabricate one of the models at full scale, documenting both its production and its completion in a short video alongside vignettes of two of the firm's realized projects, a low-cost housing project and a restaurant, both in Mexico City. Emphasizing construction processes and also shifting perceptions of realized form, Michan's video provides carefully framed glimpses of the interplay of materials, light, surface, and space. The goal is to guide viewers as they "travel through matter and form, texture and ornament" to experience "the conceptual drivers" of his work and "the unexpected expressions that develop as a result."

Eschewing the virtual domain for the physical, New Affiliates principals Ivi Diamantopoulou and Jaffer Kolb decided to "get dirty and make something in the ground." They constructed *Roof Cuttings*, five compact pavilions in community gardens across New York City. Asking "What is the smallest architectural gesture that can produce some value?" the designers used Abbé Laugier's primitive hut to identify the essential elements for these structures, provisions for shelter and rest. The garden buildings were constructed with scavenged greenhouse sheathing and aluminum siding. Extensively documented and mapped on downloadable handouts, the shelters, as imagined by Diamantopoulou and Kolb, could potentially form "part of a larger roof, dispersed over New York's five boroughs . . . a funny set whose value shifts between the individual and the collective; the moment and the aggregate."

Vrtical partners Luis Beltrán del Río García and Andrew Sosa Martínez produced five videos that explore their design philosophy and projects: a temple, an artisans' market, a sculptor's "haven," and a modernist renovation. The designers write that given the "impossibility of creating a physical exhibition where drawings, models, and photographs would do the job," they view storytelling as the best means to help audiences imagine the experiences that "occur throughout the lifespan of a design." In each short video, a narrator speaks as a blocky pixelated composition slowly comes into focus, providing room for the viewer to "build the rest of the architecture in their own mind." Through this experience, the partners hope to convey how each project illustrates "the values we hold dear and the profession we cherish."

The League Prize theme provided a remarkably prescient call to action during what proved to be an extraordinary season of confinement, displacement, and social reckoning. With the statement "In its many forms, value demonstrates a stance toward the wider world, influencing how we act, sense, imagine, and create, both collectively and individually," the competition brief challenged entrants to extend beyond individual projects and practices to a broader conception of working with and within their communities.

opposite: Architectural
League Prize
2020 Call for Entries
Design: Pentagram

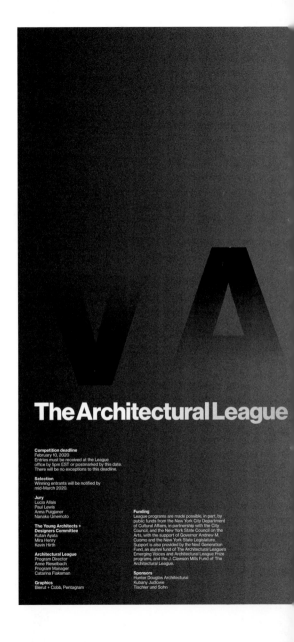

The Architectural League

Competition deadline
February 10, 2020
Entries must be received at the League
office by 5pm EST or postmarked by this date.
There will be no exceptions to this deadline.

Selection
Winning entrants will be notified by
mid-March 2020.

Jury
Lucia Allais
Paul Lewis
Anna Puigjaner
Nanako Umemoto

**The Young Architects +
Designers Committee**
Kutan Ayata
Mira Henry
Kevin Hirth

Architectural League
Program Director
Anne Rieselbach
Program Manager
Catarina Flaksman

Graphics
Bierut + Cobb, Pentagram

Funding
League programs are made possible, in part, by
public funds from the New York City Department
of Cultural Affairs, in partnership with the City
Council, and the New York State Council on the
Arts, with the support of Governor Andrew M.
Cuomo and the New York State Legislature.
Support is also provided by the Next Generation
Fund, an alumni fund of The Architectural League's
Emerging Voices and Architectural League Prize
programs, and the J. Clawson Mills Fund of The
Architectural League.

Sponsors
Hunter Douglas Architectural
Kubany Judlowe
Tischler und Sohn

Call for entries
Young architects and designers are invited to submit work to the annual Architectural League Prize Competition. Projects of all types, either theoretical or real, and executed in any medium, are welcome. The jury will select work for presentation in lectures, digital media, and an exhibition in June 2020. Winners will receive a cash prize of $2,000.

Established in 1981 to recognize visionary work by young practitioners, the Architectural League Prize is an annual competition, lecture series, and exhibition organized by The Architectural League and its Young Architects + Designers Committee. For more information about The Architectural League and work by past winners, please visit archleague.org/leagueprize.

Eligibility
The competition is open only to current full-time residents (who need not be citizens) of the United States, Canada, and Mexico. Entrants must be ten years or less out of a bachelor's or master's degree program. Current students are ineligible. Complete eligibility requirements, including information on partnerships and collaborative work, can be found at archleague.org/competition/lp20.

Theme: Value
Value is a slippery construct in architecture, leading to thoughts of numbers, colors, measurement, worth, and ethics. Value can be personal or shared, analytical or sensorial. It suggests economic and aesthetic highs and lows and hints at the ideological urgencies that undergird and influence the production of architecture. In its many forms, value demonstrates a stance toward the wider world, influencing how we act, sense, imagine, and create, both collectively and individually.

In a time of political and social precariousness when all cultural value sets seem publicly permissible, this year's Architectural League Prize competition asks how notions of value operate in your work. How are your values mediated by the processes of design? What are the discursive contexts, forms of representation, and/or spaces of action in which these values manifest themselves?

Submission requirements
A single printed portfolio, which may include several projects, must be bound and no larger than 11" × 14". The portfolio may not contain more than thirty double-sided pages. Digital materials will not be accepted.

The competition theme is given as a basis for young architects and designers to reflect upon and reevaluate their work. A written statement not to exceed 250 words is required, which defines and considers the work under the rubric of the competition theme. Significant weight is given to how an applicant's work addresses the theme. The written statement must be on the first page of the portfolio.

Entries must be received at the League office by 5pm EST February 10, 2020, or postmarked by that date. Entries should be delivered to 594 Broadway, Suite 607, New York, NY 10012.

Entry fee
Each entrant must submit an entry fee of $35. Entrants may pay the fee online via the competition page on archleague.org/competition/lp20 or include cash or a check payable to The Architectural League of New York with their submission. If paying online, please be sure that the credit card is in the name of one of the entrants; we are unable to accept payments made on behalf of others.

Entry forms
Each entrant must submit two versions of the entry form, one online on archleague.org/competition/lp20 and one copy included with the submission. Insert the completed hardcopy form into an unsealed envelope attached to the inside back cover of the submission. To maintain anonymity, no identification of the entrant may appear on any part of the submission, except on the entry form and return envelope (see below).

Portfolio return
Portfolios will be returned by mail only if a self-addressed envelope with prepaid postage or a label is also enclosed. Please ensure that return postage does not expire before August 2020. The Architectural League assumes no liability for original drawings. The League will take every precaution to return submissions intact, but can assume no responsibility for loss or damage. Portfolios may be discarded after one year if no return envelope is provided.

ze for Young **Architects + Designers 2020**

KUBANY JUDLOWE

Biographies

David Eskenazi / d.esk
Los Angeles, California

d.esk is led by David Eskenazi in Los Angeles. Current projects are in California and Mexico. Alongside the practice, Eskenazi writes and teaches. His essays have appeared in *Log, Project, Offramp,* and *Pidgin*. He has been awarded the Oberdick Fellowship at the University of Michigan, the LeFevre Fellowship at the Ohio State University, and a MacDowell Fellowship.

Eskenazi holds an MArch from SCI-Arc and a BArch from Carnegie Mellon University. Currently, he is a member of the design studio and visual studies faculty at SCI-Arc.

Garrett Ricciardi and Julian Rose / Formlessfinder
Brooklyn, New York / Los Angeles, California

Formlessfinder was established by Garrett Ricciardi and Julian Rose in New York in 2010. The studio, now based in Brooklyn and Los Angeles, pursues a wide range of theoretical and real-world projects, from residential and commercial projects to public pavilions and installations. The foundation of Formlessfinder's approach to architecture is the exploration of new design methodologies and the implementation of collaborations that reach beyond the field's traditional boundaries: conversations with physicists and materials scientists have led to construction with loose sand, while an ongoing exchange with experts in historic preservation has given rise to a series of theoretical studies and publications.

Formlessfinder has received numerous design awards including the AIA NY New Practices award, a National Endowment for the Arts project grant, and Design Miami's Design Visionary Award. The studio was also a finalist for the MoMA/PS1 Young Architects Program. Formlessfinder's work has been exhibited at the Venice Biennale, MAXXI in Rome, the Art Institute of Chicago, Design Miami, the Chicago Architecture Biennial, and the Museum of Modern Art in New York. The partners are the editors of *Formless*, Storefront for Art and Architecture Manifesto Series 1.

Ricciardi and Rose received MArch degrees from Princeton University, where Ricciardi was awarded the Suzanne Kolarik Underwood Prize and Rose was awarded the History and Theory Prize. Prior to attending Princeton, Ricciardi completed the Whitney Independent Study Program and received his BFA from the Cooper Union. Rose received his BA from Harvard University. Ricciardi currently teaches at the UCLA School of Architecture, and Rose and Ricciardi have taught together at Columbia University and Princeton University.

Leslie Lok, Sasa Zivkovic / HANNAH
Ithaca, New York

HANNAH is an experimental design and research studio that works across scales, from furniture to buildings to urbanism. Founded by Leslie Lok and Sasa Zivkovic in 2014, the office has a keen interest in architectural explorations grounded in material expression, digital fabrication, and construction. HANNAH's recent work includes the 3D-printed *RRRolling Stones* furniture at Socrates Sculpture Park in Long Island City, New York; *A New Robotic Brutalism—Additive Architectural Elements*, a solo exhibition at Pinkcomma Gallery in Boston; and *Ashen Cabin*, a robotically fabricated building in Ithaca, New York.

HANNAH was named one of *Architect Magazine*'s Next Progressives in 2018 and won ArchDaily's Best New Practice Award in 2021. The studio's work has been published in *Architectural Record, Architect Magazine, Log,* the *New York Times, Dwell,* and *Dezeen,* among others. Zivkovic's and Lok's academic research has been widely published in book chapters and at peer-reviewed conferences.

Lok and Zivkovic are assistant professors of architecture at Cornell University's College of Architecture, Art, and Planning. Lok directs the Rural-Urban Building Innovation (RUBI) Laboratory, which investigates new building methods that couple digital construction technologies with natural and non-standardized material for the design of adaptable buildings and housing in rural-urban contexts. Zivkovic directs the Robotic Construction Laboratory (RCL), a research group that focuses on the development of sustainable robotic construction technologies to advance the future built environment. Lok and Zivkovic received MArch degrees from the Massachusetts Institute of Technology.

Isaac Michan Daniel / Michan Architecture
Mexico City, Mexico

Michan Architecture, founded in 2010, is based in Mexico City. The studio operates as a laboratory of architecture, exploring new possibilities within the discipline. The practice considers architecture to be a flirtation toward a built environment, a speculation of what the future might be.

The work of the studio ranges from temporary installations to commercial spaces to large-scale residential projects. It has been featured in multiple publications and exhibitions and has received numerous awards. In 2019, Michan received the Design Vanguard award from *Architectural Record*. The AL Apartment received the 2017 American Architecture Prize in Residential Architecture, and the Z53 Low-Cost Housing project won a 2015 Architizer Award for affordable housing.

Isaac Michan Daniel leads the practice. He holds a BArch from Universidad Iberoamericana with studies at RMIT University and an MS in Architecture from Pratt Institute. He has taught at Universidad Anáhuac, Universidad Iberoamericana, and the AA Visiting School in Mexico City.

Ivi Diamantopoulou, Jaffer Kolb / New Affiliates
New York, New York

New Affiliates, based in New York, is an award-winning design practice led by Ivi Diamantopoulou and Jaffer Kolb. Since founding the practice in 2016, Diamantopoulou and Kolb have completed a range of work, from ground-up projects to interiors to exhibitions and installations. The office uses building to reconsider how architecture is practiced, both as a service profession and as a site of material production.

In addition to commissioned work, New Affiliates initiates projects and investigations that focus on matters of reuse within a context of material excess, particularly under current standards of practice. For this work, they have collaborated with the City of New York Department of Sanitation and the New York City Department of Parks and Recreation, among other municipal bodies.

New Affiliates' work has been published in *Architect Magazine, Metropolis, Cultured Magazine,* and *Wallpaper* and shown at the Canadian Centre for Architecture, Storefront for Art and Architecture, Performa 19, and elsewhere. In 2020, the studio was recognized by the AIA NY as a winner of the New Practices New York competition.

Diamantopoulou received an MArch from Princeton University and a Diploma in Architecture and Engineering from the University of Patras in Greece. Kolb received an MArch from Princeton University, an MS in Urban Planning from the London School of Economics, and a BA from Wesleyan University.

Luis Beltrán del Río García, Andrew Sosa Martínez / Vrtical
Mexico City, Mexico

Vrtical, a design workshop dedicated to making architecture more accessible to multiple audiences, was founded in 2014 by architects Luis Beltrán del Río García and Andrew Sosa Martínez. The studio adapts methods and processes to meet clients' spatial needs in different contexts and at different scales and also addresses aesthetics and functionality of space as keys to a better life.

Luis Beltrán del Río García graduated from the National Autonomous University of Mexico and has a master's degree in urban management for developing countries from the Technical University of Berlin. In his work, he seeks to balance a pragmatic practice and a strong academic viewpoint. He has taught project workshops at UNAM, TU Berlin, Centro de diseño, cine y televisión, and Universidad Anáhuac, and he has collaborated with the Pontifical Catholic University of Chile.

Andrew Sosa Martínez received his degree from Universidad Anáhuac. He has taught design workshops at Universidad Anáhuac and Centro de diseño, cine y televisión.

David Eskenazi

d.esk

d.esk makes and learns and experiments and fails, over and over and over again. We use paper, compare things, and design buildings through both open-ended inquiry and commissioned projects. Our work begins with long-standing conundrums or assumptions having to do with architectural form, and then we tease out alternatives. We choose tape over glue, tone over hue, coherence over style, the abrupt over the transitional, creativity through convention, the soft and the hard, things provisional over things fixed, and over or, the strange over the weird, subtlety over obviousness, the considered over the neglected, the now over the new, cheapness as luxury, and alliance over commitment. The practice values good taste, deep thought, and ethical imagination.

Inhale, Exhale, Sag, Flex

Los Angeles, California, 2020

The public bath house is an urban utility that produces an aura of the collective. While the primary function is to clean and relax a person, it is also a space where strangers care for themselves in a manner that is both personal and social. And like the bodies it houses, the architecture is continuously soiled, sanitized, and maintained.

We designed this flexible, easily fabricated, demountable bath house for city-owned lots in Los Angeles. The proposal consists of two buildings separated by a stair. An expanding quilt of water bladders, which fill as steam evaporates and bodies exhale, encloses *Flex*, the steam house. A frame structure wrapped in building paper supports *Sag*, the pool house. The paper is removed, dried, and reinstalled once it absorbs too many pool splashes and too much shower steam. Both buildings are interior landscapes of curtains, pipes, water, steam, plunges, and bodies, where architecture and people disrobe and self-care.

Project team: Julie Riley

opposite: Pool view

below: Rendered
section through
sauna and main pool

bottom left: Rendered
section through sauna
and bathrooms

bottom right:
Steam room

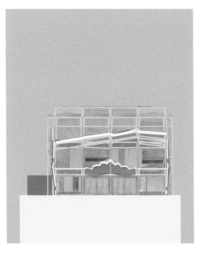

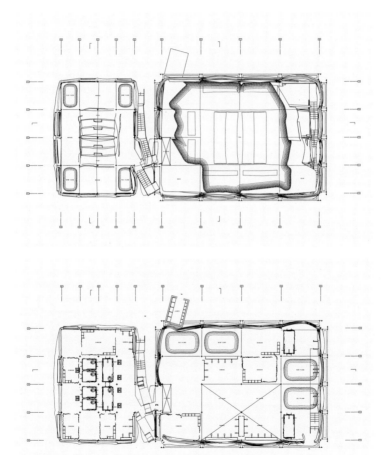

Two Scrolls
2019

Two Scrolls compares the forms of two proposed buildings. The project attempts to mix the material properties of a physical model with the intangible properties of a digital model. The scrolls propose buildings that are different sizes—45 feet high and 9 feet high—but the models are the same size. The models mix printed digital simulations, slumped paper, and tape.

Project team: Julie Riley, Jixun Wen

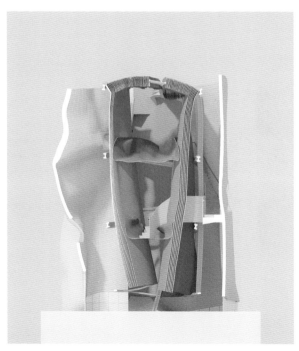

left: Rendered section of 45-foot scroll

opposite: Adjustable form at two scales

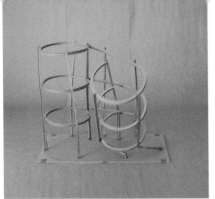

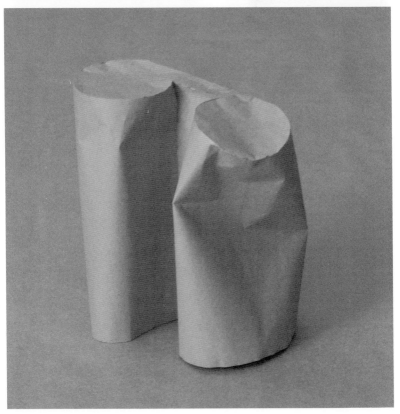

opposite top:
Structure and form tests of 3-foot scroll

opposite bottom:
Form test of 9-inch scroll

below and bottom left:
Interior structure and exterior of 9-foot scroll

below and bottom right:
Interior structure and exterior of 45-foot scroll

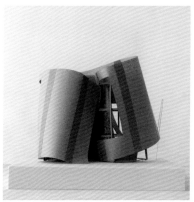

Ziggurhut
Yucatán, Mexico, 2018–ongoing

This house is located on the Yucatán peninsula in Mexico, close to the ruins of Mayan cities and also to the spot where the dinosaur-killing asteroid hit the earth. One site evidences a regional ancestry while the other records a global calamity. Our interest encompasses both the idea of local culture and the development of global forms.

Our proposal is a house-city in the jungle: two three-tiered buildings that appear to have landed haphazardly within an enclosed garden. The structures recall the Mayan stepped pyramid, a form found in many prehistoric cultures. The larger form is a two-story, one-bedroom house; the smaller is one story with two guest bedrooms. The doors to each house are the same size, while the windows are in proportion to the overall volumes.

The garden, which occupies a corner of the site, is the center of life in the house-city. All three bedrooms open directly to the planted area. An outdoor shower and two fireplaces extend into the garden from the perimeter wall like figures in the background of the city. We envision the members of a large family and the community of neighbors moving in and out of the little city.

Project Team: Joshua Coronado, Dutra Brown

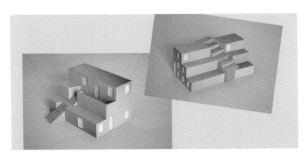

left: Model views of houses

opposite top: View across pool toward large house

opposite bottom: Model view of houses and garden

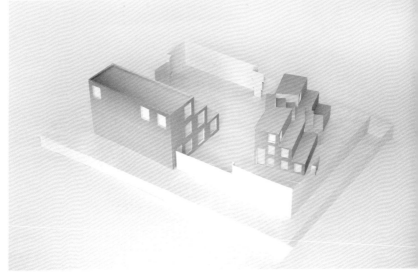

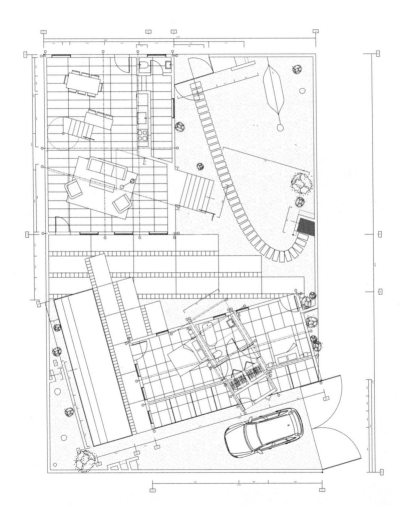

below and center: Detail views of house under construction

bottom left: Three-tiered form in two sizes

bottom right: Model elevations

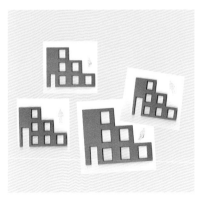
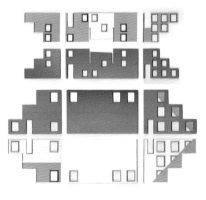

Slump Model
Wedge Gallery
Woodbury University, Los Angeles, California, 2019

This installation presents a model of the two identical facades of Ziggurhut at 1:2 scale. At this size, Ziggurhut fits perfectly into the trapezoidal plan of Woodbury University's Wedge Gallery. The techniques and logic of the model's construction are more commonly found at a much smaller scale, leading to the model's deformation and collapse. Ultimately, the installation is a proposal for a new kind of architectural resistance that dodges the upright, the strong, and the geometric.

Project Team: Jixun Wen

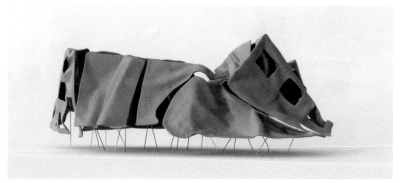

below: Installation view

bottom: *Slump Model* elevation superimposed on Ziggurhut elevations

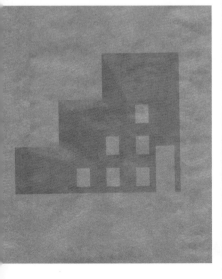

Training Wheels
Banvard Gallery
Ohio State University, Columbus, Ohio, 2015

Big things often seem more serious than small things. Big things are more weighty, more in the way, more noticeable, more aggravating. They just seem more real. Small things, on the other hand, are easily brushed aside and forgotten, as though they were never there. This installation aspires to make something big seem as insignificant as something small.

An installation of architecture presents itself as something big. It wants to be taken seriously—like a building, a serious big thing. But installations are limited by their size and their clear difference from building: they can only desire to be big and serious. In this installation, we made that desire manifest in the tension between the many large wheels and their model-like materiality.

The wheels are made of cardboard, cheap yet strong. Cardboard makes good models but not very good buildings. The physicality of the cardboard emphasizes that the larger-than-a-person objects have the qualities of an overscaled model. Furthermore, the wheels are staged like large drawings, sharing a consistent scale in geometry, notation, material, and concept.

Although big things usually suggest stability, these wheels can roll into almost any configuration. They are lightweight and available for rearrangement at any time. The suggestion of mutability put forth by the assemblage of wheels is just that— a suggestion—since the gallery is only slightly larger than the collection. Additionally, the geometry of the wheels is off—kinks in the circles, askew centers of gravity— constraining them to rocking rather than rolling. Instead of implying a sense of infinite movement, these wheels suggest only a slight disruption from a stable location.

Project Team: Alex Mann, Amanda Pierce

right: Installation view

bottom: Views of individual wheel

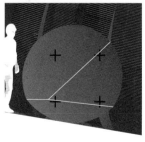

opposite:
Installation view

below: Elevation

bottom left:
Installation view

bottom right:
Wheels drawn together

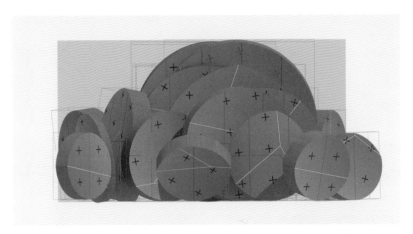

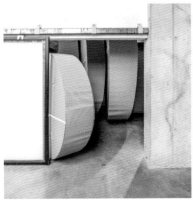

Colossal Paper
Proposed Monument for Abu Simbel, Egypt
2019

A surprise: while 3D printing a scan of *Slump Model* after the installation closed, we were struck by its resemblance to an 1850 photograph taken in Egypt by Maxime du Camp. The plastic formwork of the 3D print recalled the photograph's featureless environment.

Our proposal for a colossal monument to this photograph mixes a scan of slumped paper; a six-inch-high, three-dimensional image of the photograph; and the required support structure. We imagine the actual monument to be 450 stories tall.

Project Team: Jixun Wen

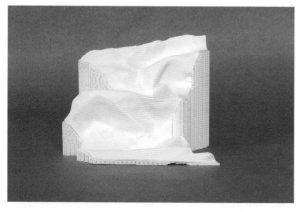

left: Paper and formwork

opposite top: Giant form, paper, and support tower

opposite bottom left: Paper, brim, giant form, and support tower

opposite bottom right: Paper, support tower, and hook support

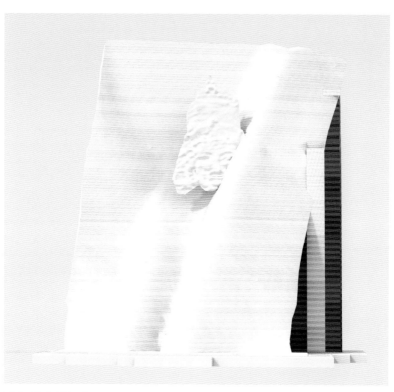

Garrett Ricciardi and Julian Rose

Formlessfinder

It's a commonplace that there are no longer any universal values: that it's all relative; that even seemingly clear-cut issues can be seen from at least two points of view; that there are, as they say, very fine people on both sides. This fracturing of values has had far-reaching political and cultural consequences, issuing a profound challenge to all dimensions of public life. It seems to pose a particularly existential problem for architecture, which is inherently collective in both production and reception. If architecture should aspire to express "the new spirit" of its age, as Le Corbusier famously proclaimed, what can architecture do in an age without a spirit?

The discipline has responded primarily with handwringing over what values to express and how to express them. Yet these debates overlook a deeper, more insidious problem. After all, it is not quite accurate to say that there are no shared values. One ubiquitous force has rushed in to fill the vacuum—the market. In the absence of consensus, market value has become de facto absolute value. And so building continues apace even as architecture is in crisis. Market forces, more than any other factor, shape the built environment worldwide. Indeed, as any design professional knows, the most frequent and consequential conversations about value take place in the context of value engineering, that exemplary euphemism invented to describe the process through which economic pressures devour an architectural idea like a school of piranhas. This economic logic reaches its apotheosis in the so-called value chains ubiquitous in management consulting and business development, which limn with relentless clarity the drive toward the cheapest and most efficient transformation of resources and labor into products and profit.

Market value is bigger than architecture—indeed, bigger than culture itself—and it would be a fool's errand for architects to try to replace it with a new new spirit. Instead of proposing a value system, then, our practice aims to implode systemic thinking itself. Architecture is often asked to represent stability, but architects have always also grappled with precarity in the most literal sense. Perhaps the time has come to recognize this as the profession's greatest asset. We see value as fluid, dynamic, and, above all, formless.

Subbiyah Highway Archaeology
and Infrastructure Research Center
Kuwait Pavilion, Venice Biennale
Venice, Italy, 2020–2021

Archaeologists commonly consider three types of value: use value (present needs), option value (future possibilities), and existence value ("because it is there").

We were asked by the curators of the Kuwait Pavilion for the 2020 Venice Biennale to envision a new strategy for coordinating archaeological exploration and infrastructure development within Kuwait's vast hinterland. This invitation came in response to a recent crisis: in 2019, construction of a new superhighway was halted by the discovery of a major archaeological site in the Kuwaiti desert.

It is widely assumed that new construction is in direct conflict with historic preservation. But our design for the Subbiyah Highway Archaeology and Infrastructure Research Center is based on the fact that, in terms of actual material and process, archaeology and construction are almost the same. They both begin with holes in the ground, and they both involve moving huge quantities of earth. Kuwait is uniquely positioned to pioneer new approaches to the preservation of its ancient sites because many of them have been unearthed only in the last half century; in many other areas of North Africa and the Middle East, important sites explored during the colonial era saw their artifacts removed to the museums of Europe and the United States.

Our proposal takes this set of circumstances as its starting point, pursuing a design strategy that is simultaneously additive and subtractive. The construction of new architecture and infrastructure above ground will balance the excavation of existing sites below ground, combining ongoing archaeological excavation with visitor access and interpretation.

opposite top:
Aerial view

opposite bottom:
Ground view

EXCAVATION

1A North portion of east trench. An archaeological dig is nearly indistinguishable from a Land Art site. Both are treasured items in the collected history of art and architecture. One is fragile and takes place under the eye of archaeologists and preservationists; the other is left at the mercy of the elements and natural entropy.

1B Since around 2015, Formlessfinder has conducted multiple research projects related to deserts in the American Southwest. We have looked at how landscape, environment, lost desert architectures, and nascent Land Art projects have shaped understanding of the region. We have considered this research alongside potential new narratives for this vast and largely uninhabited region of the United States.

TRANSPORTATION

2A Typical highways (in any region) are deemed to be little more than the most efficient, simple, and banal structures on the planet. We see highways rather as highly dynamic assemblies brimming with design potential. They are part infrastructure, part natural history, part never-ending flow of human stories and materials.

2B Our Los Angeles office sits amid a tangle of urban and desert highways, part of one of the most ambitious infrastructural and land alteration projects in the world. The post–World War II structures both redefined growth and grappled with the transformation of historic neighborhoods and fragile ecologies.

TOOLS

3A Although different in scale and brute force, the archaeologist's spade is remarkably similar in form to the civil engineer's bulldozer.

3B Many Formlessfinder projects have required us to explore construction strategies that are more typically used for infrastructure and landscape than for conventional forms of architecture. Since roughly 2010, this has included collaborations with contractors for the Army Corps of Engineers and suppliers to the mining industry.

MATERIALS

4A Ashlar in fine beach rock, excavated 1960–1963. Artifact, material, architectural massing— all three or somewhere in between?

4B We have looked to the processes of analyzing ground composition not only as a preliminary step for establishing placement and sizing foundations but as providing final materials for our designs. Core samples can be used to determine the ground makeup below a structure, but they are just as likely to become a finished design—for example, a stool that is as durable as the earth itself.

Tent Pile
Design Miami
Miami, Florida, 2013

Globally, fifty billion tons of sand are consumed every year. It is the most used natural resource besides air and water. The market cost of sand ranges from about 5 to 30 dollars per ton; the environmental and human cost of global sand extraction and consumption is incalculable. The construction industry goes through 90 percent of the sand used each year.

Tent Pile is architecture that went from nothing to something and back to nothing. It hovered somewhere between building and infrastructure; it was constructed and recycled with virtually zero waste. After we were selected to design the entry pavilion for the 2013 Design Miami fair, we delved into the local geography and architectural history of the region. On the one hand, sand is ubiquitous—any kind of construction in Miami must take into account this loose and shifting substrate. On the other hand, a primary typology of vernacular architecture in Miami is the public space that emerged from the collision between an exuberant postwar modernism and the tropical climate: hybrid indoor/outdoor spaces that are sheltered by dramatically cantilevered roofs yet not enclosed by walls, that simultaneously offer shelter and free and fluid access.

Our design mediated between the mass and looseness of sand and the lightness and precision of cantilever design. An enormous pile of sand—left unfixed for the duration of the installation—provided the foundation for a 30-foot-long cantilevered roof consisting of trusses CNC-milled from solid plates of aluminum. After the pavilion hosted more than 50,000 visitors, the roof was recycled and the sand was donated to coastal restoration efforts nearby.

opposite: Pavilion views

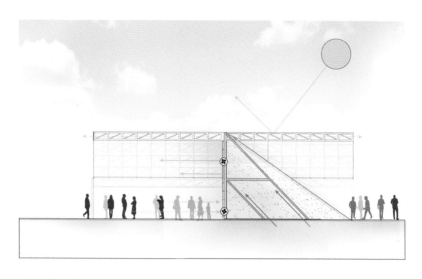

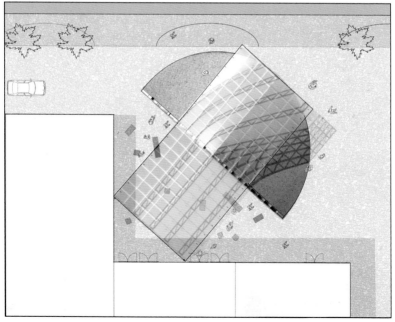

opposite top: Thermal diagram of sand pile

below left: Sand pile and truss detail

bottom: Night view

opposite bottom: Plan

below right: Interior view

50 Seats in 50 States

2018–ongoing

The $18-trillion US economy relies on a vast network of infrastructure, from roads and bridges to freight rail and ports to electric grids and internet provision. But the systems currently in place were, for the most part, built decades ago, and economists say that delays and rising maintenance costs are limiting productivity and performance.

Core Drill seating is the first prototype in our Land Art National Park research and design project. We intend to drill—from a defunct piece of infrastructure or a depleted natural resource—one seat from each of the 50 states. These seats will construct a new narrative about the country's resource chains, questioning current policies of land use and acquisition. While such raw materials are typically hidden behind and within architectural surfaces, our project presents them as matter and as fact. The first prototype was drilled from an obsolete bridge structure in Queens, New York, and exhibited at the Storefront for Art and Architecture in the summer of 2018.

opposite: Land Art National Park annual report

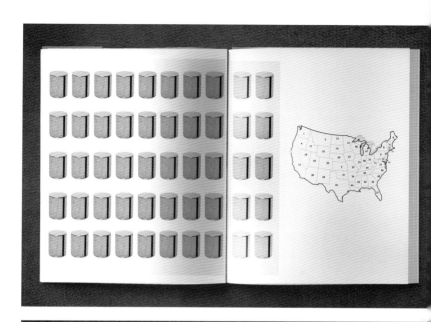

WastED at Blue Hill

New York, New York, 2015

According to the Food and Agriculture Organization of the United Nations, an estimated 1.4 billion tons of food, roughly 30 percent of global production, is lost or wasted annually.

We worked with Dan Barber, the award-winning chef behind Blue Hill at Stone Barns in Pocantico Hills, New York, and Blue Hill in Manhattan, on WastED, a pop-up restaurant devoted to creating world-class food sourced entirely from food and farm "waste." Our design was inspired in equal parts by the extraordinary creativity of the menu, which included dishes like edible beef-tallow candles and salads made from vegetable peels, and by our visits to the agricultural and culinary facilities at Stone Barns. The core ambition driving both the architecture and the food was to transform material that would otherwise be ignored, undervalued, or discarded into something unexpectedly beautiful and/or delicious.

WastED aimed to rethink materials and ingredients at every point in the supply chain and at every step in the manufacturing process, from the harvesting of raw materials (grain for pasta, hardwood for furniture) to the economics of shipping and transportation. The design focused on two basic elements: a wall covering made of agricultural fabric (the same material used to cover crops inside the Stone Barns greenhouses) and custom tabletops grown from fungus and corn husk scraps.

below: Interior view

bottom center:
Crop cover

bottom right:
Detail of crop cover

bottom left: Crops

WastED at Selfridges

London, United Kingdom, 2017

Research shows that 7.2 million tons of household food waste is thrown away each year in the United Kingdom. Almost three quarters of that amount—nearly 5 tons—is food that could have been eaten.

After the success of WastED at Blue Hill in New York, we embarked on a second collaboration with chef Dan Barber, this time for a pop-up restaurant in a rooftop space at the flagship Selfridges store in the heart of London. We interpreted the WastED concept through the tradition of the English garden, a place where unfiltered nature, agriculture, and storytelling come together. Our WastED rooftop garden explored the narratives behind the ingredients, sources, and processes of food waste. Guests were invited to explore this garden-exhibition before, during, and after their meal; chefs and servers drew from the WastED content to create a unique experience that is part meal and part performance.

CASE #1
Wool

CASE #2
Tilet Trimmings

CASE #3
Jamón Bone

CASE #4
Artichoke Thistle

CASE #5
Cascara Husk

CASE #6
Waste Napkins

CASE #7
Fruit Juice Runoff

CASE #8
Bone Char

opposite: Exhibition guide   **below left:** WastED vitrine   **below right:** Vegetable-dyed textile   **bottom:** Video corridor

Artforum **Bookstore at Comme des Garçons**
New York, New York, 2014–2015

Approximately 300 million tons of paper are produced around the world each year. The average American uses more than 700 pounds annually. In the United States, paper accounts for 25 percent of landfill waste and 33 percent of municipal waste.

Many of New York's significant buildings are masonry structures, which are held upright by their mass of bricks or stone blocks and the force of gravity. Our bookstore for *Artforum* and Comme des Garçons' Dover Street Market, located inside Harvey Wiley Corbett's New York School of Applied Design for Women (1908), itself constructed of brick and stone, picks up on this centuries-old tradition.

We transformed more than 10,000 pounds of unsold magazines destined for the recycle bin into walls of self-supporting, interlocking, masonry-esque units. The project and partnership mark the first in a series of ongoing collaborations between the two brands. Unique spaces created by bringing art, fashion, and design together display current and vintage issues from *Artforum*'s rich archive.

opposite top:
Bookcase

opposite bottom left:
Corner stacking detail

opposite bottom right:
Corner strap detail

opposite: Bookstore interior

below: Structural model of magazine masonry unit

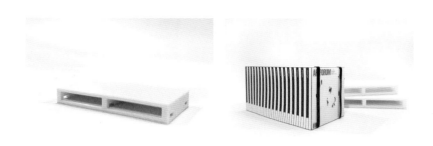

Leslie Lok and Sasa Zivkovic

HANNAH

Digital design and fabrication technologies are intrinsic to the making of our work from the ground up, facilitating new material methods, tectonic articulations, environmental practices, technological affordances, spatial assemblies, and forms of construction. At HANNAH, we build and embrace shared value with the help of self-created and open-source construction machines. These principles, we argue, inevitably affect how we think and design through making. We aim to mine the tension between machine means and architectural ends while also reclaiming authorship over processes of construction that influence the way we build—or perhaps ought to build in the future.

The performance and the architectural expression of our work are derived from materiality, digital construction protocols, robotic routines, and bottom-up design logics. At the same time, in a mix of means, the projects are inspired by precedent, program, ecological considerations, collective labor, personal obsessions, and the misuse of technology. In *Ashen Cabin*, irregularly shaped and bug-infested "waste wood" is transformed into an available, affordable, and morbidly sustainable building material for the Anthropocene. In *RRRolling Stones*, the ability of the 3D printer to mass-customize geometries economically is utilized to create seats that are tailored for a variety of body types. In *A New Robotic Brutalism—Additive Architectural Elements*, 3D printing concrete eliminates wasteful formwork and prompts the reemergence of corbelling, an anachronistic structural and spatial strategy. In *Fabricate Lilong*, generative urban strategies are derived from the logics of 3D-printed construction. In *Log Knot*, computational optimization protocols enable complex curvatures to be constructed with raw material and minimal formwork. In Open Source Factory, the collective hacking of machinery facilitates creative access to otherwise prohibitively costly large-scale fabrication equipment.

As designers, we consider ourselves to be biased generalists rather than intensive specialists. Our projects reject any dogmatism from machine-derived means by combining different methods of making, material applications, geometries, environmental frameworks, and social narratives. Together, the various and sometimes conflicting means and methods—robotic and otherwise—inform how we create architectural expression and value.

Ashen Cabin

Ithaca, New York, 2019

Ashen Cabin is a three-by-three-meter building 3D-printed from concrete and clothed in a robotically fabricated envelope of irregular ash logs. All concrete components were manufactured on a large-scale, self-built 3D printer by means of a custom printing process and using corbelling as a design strategy. The structure has three programmatic areas — table, storage seat, and 6.5-meter-tall fireplace — and is elevated on concrete legs that adjust to the sloped terrain.

The envelope consists of wood infested by the emerald ash borer, widely considered to be waste wood or firewood. Our high-precision 3D scanning and fabrication technology upcycles irregularly shaped and EAB-infested "waste" into a sustainable building material, challenging preconceived notions about material standards in wood and timber construction.

Ashen Cabin walks the line between familiar and unfamiliar, between technologically advanced and formally elemental. The undulating wood surfaces accentuate the program of the building yet recall the natural log geometry they are derived from, while the curvature of the wood highlights moments of architectural importance, such as windows, entrances, roofs, and canopies.

Project Team: Byungchan Ahn, Christopher Battaglia, Kun Bi, Jeremy Bilotti, Elie Boutros, Isabel Branas Jarque, Sarah Bujnowski, Reuben Chen, Freddo Daneshvaran, Ethan Davis, Ramses Gonzalez, Brian Havener, Justin Hazelwood, Eleanor Krause, Lingzhe Lu, Xiaoxue Iris Ma, Alexandre Mecattaf, Todd Petrie, Mitchie Qiao, Russell Southard, Alexander Terry, Dax Simitch Warke, Jiaying Wei, Jiayi Xing, Xiaohang Yan, Jingxin Yang, Wangda Zhu

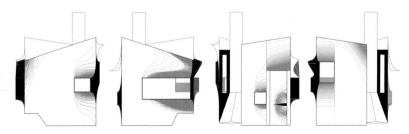

top left: Detail view of large south-facing window with roof drainage scupper

bottom left: Detail view of transition between 3D-printed concrete leg and chimney

right: Initial facade mock-up consisting of robotically sliced bent ash logs

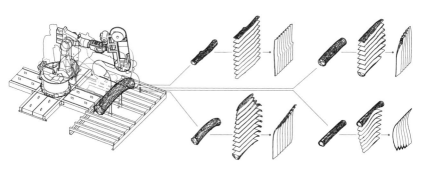

Leslie Lok and Sasa Zivkovic **75**

RRRolling Stones
The Architectural League/Socrates Sculpture Park Folly/
Function 2018 Competition Entry
Queens, New York, 2018

RRRolling across the meadows of Socrates Sculpture Park in Queens, New York, are 25 3D-printed concrete *Stones*. These follies, winner of an annual competition held by the sculpture park and The Architectural League of New York, are both smooth and jagg(er)ed, with each turn revealing a new seating profile to accommodate different body types and sizes. Movement itself becomes a folly as park visitors discover new seating configurations with every turn.

The *RRRolling Stones* can form a single continuous bench, several smaller seating objects, or solitary compositions. The seats were fabricated with a large-scale, open-source 3D printer. Their overall shapes reference common chair archetypes, and the layered fabrication creates a textured seating surface.

Project Team: Christopher Battaglia, Kun Chen, Olivier Ducharme, Wachira Leangtanom, Jingjing Liu, Alexandre Mecattaf, Todd Petrie, Burak Unel, Anuntachai Vongvanij

Leslie Lok and Sasa Zivkovic **79**

below and center left: Installation views

bottom left: Detail of a *Stone* with interior gravel surface

bottom right: Concrete 3D printing process

opposite: Conceptual transformations of *RRRolling Stones* elevations

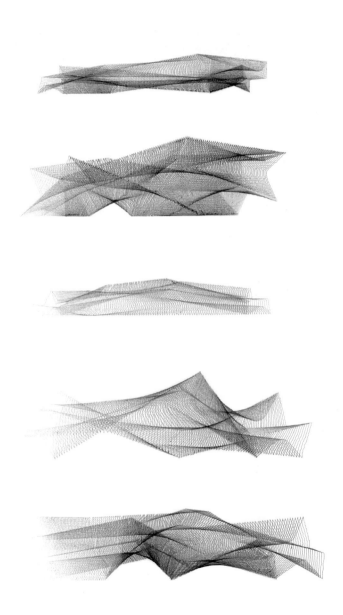

A New Robotic Brutalism—
Additive Architectural Elements
2017

The 3D printer—a Cartesian machine long defined as characterless—is in fact highly distinctive: it has integrity, personality, limitations, and formal rigor. *Additive Architectural Elements* aims to reveal the printer's idiosyncratic tectonics and narratives. For instance, the seemingly advanced technology unexpectedly promotes obsolete or archaic structural methods such as corbelling. Other strategies deployed to manipulate concrete form include changes in printing direction (upside-down or in section) to overcome printer deficiencies, revision of G-code for smart material deposit, and mass-customized alteration of geometries for structural reasons. Choosing common architectural motifs, such as floors, columns, doors, windows, walls, and ceilings, the design-research project shows how the layering of concrete, the relentless linear extrusion of material, and the act of corbelling put forward new strategies for building and create a unique architectural language of 3D-printed concrete.

Project Team: Christopher Battaglia, Jeremy Bilotti, Reuben Chen, Stephen Clond, Ainslie Cullen, Gary Esposito, Justin Foo, Charisse Fu, Jessica Jiang, Alexandre Mecattaf, Hanxi Wang

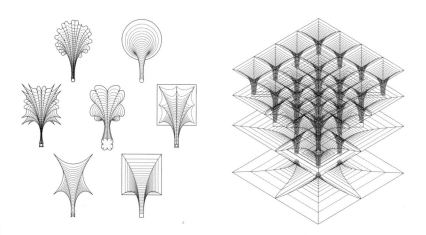

opposite left: Column element variations   **opposite right:** Proto-architectural assembly   **below:** Detail view of Column element   **bottom:** Full-scale 3D prints of the seven architectural elements

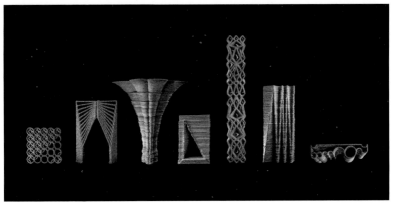

below left: Detail of Forced Column element

below right: Smart Poché Wall

below center left: Detail of underside of Column element

bottom left: Detail of Column element

bottom right: Detail of Forced Column proto-architectural PLA model

opposite: Proto-architectural models of Column and Doornament elements

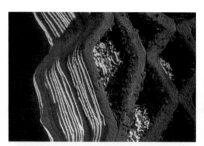

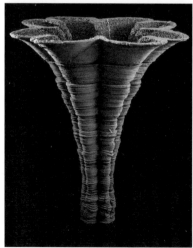

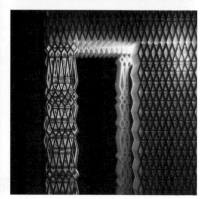

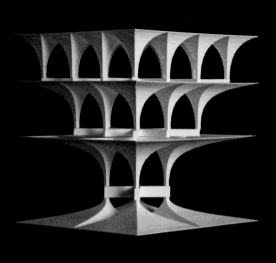

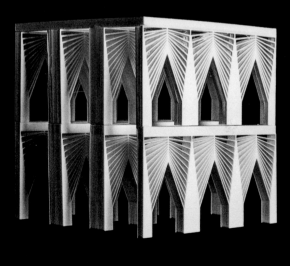

Fabricate Lilong
Shanghai, China, 2019

This project investigates the *lilong*, a housing typology specific to Shanghai. Like many traditional residential forms, it is threatened by the proliferation of modernist housing towers across China. But the *lilong*, a form of low-rise mat urbanism, has the potential to provide an alternate model for urban habitation, one that reintroduces the sociospatial dimensions often eradicated in complexes consisting of residential high-rises.

Fabricate Lilong redesigns the low-rise *lilong* at both typological and urban scales. Working with building components in layered assemblies, the project leverages the customization potential of concrete 3D printing to synthesize programmatic, spatial, and structural considerations. For example, the design utilizes the strategy of corbelling to create window and entry openings, manipulates concrete density for structural optimization, and modulates architectural poché for distinct programmatic arrangements and circulation.

For larger-scale residential development, wedge-shaped *lilong* modules are clustered to produce a variety of urban configurations with a floor area ratio comparable to that of residential tower complexes. The project reconfigures the *lilong*'s traditional spine organization into a woven network of alleys and courtyards for public and private activities.

Project Team: Rural-Urban Building Innovation (RUBI) Laboratory, Cornell University: Oonagh Davis, Yicheng Jia, Zoey Zheru Zhou

below: Streetscape and external entrance stair   **bottom:** Section through housing cluster

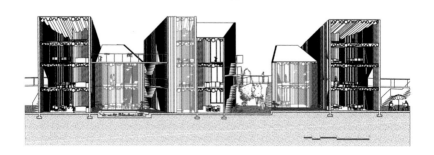

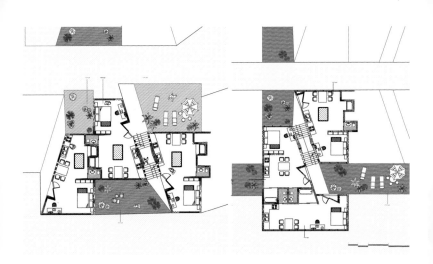

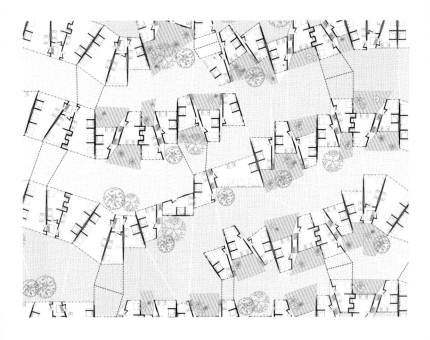

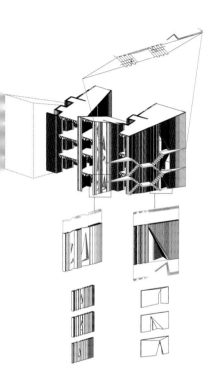

Log Knot
2018 CCA Biennial
Cornell University, Ithaca, New York, 2018

An infinitely looping, robotically fabricated architectural installation made from discarded timber, *Log Knot* provides a playful space for the Cornell campus community. The project references both the eternal cycle of birth, growth, and decay intrinsic to forest ecosystems and the coincident interdependencies between natural and technological systems. The mathematically defined figure-eight *Log Knot* borrows strategies from traditional wood craft and manufacturing and aims to expand and take best advantage of natural trees in construction. With robotic-based fabrication and high-resolution 3D scanning, the process we developed for *Log Knot* is able to utilize irregularly shaped "waste" roundwood. The project promotes reciprocating synergies and feedback among material usage, fabrication, digital form, and full-scale construction.

Unfamiliar notions of craftsmanship and precision, both digital and analogue, emerge from *Log Knot*'s conceptual design practice and construction technique. The curving, knotted network fosters an engaging interaction between natural timber geometry, computation, structural optimization, and robotic fabrication. By questioning how forest resources are used, *Log Knot* provides critical commentary on wood cycles beyond the ecosystem.

Project Team: Robotic Construction Laboratory (RCL), Cornell University: Edward Aguilera Perez, Angel Almanzar, Christopher Battaglia, Isabel Branas Jarque, Stephen Clond, Brian Havener, Cait McCarthy, Alexandre Mecattaf, Todd Petrie, Alexander Terry, Kashyap Valiveti, Dax Simitch Warke, Jordan Young

opposite top:
Installation on lawn
of Cornell Ag Quad

opposite bottom:
Aerial view

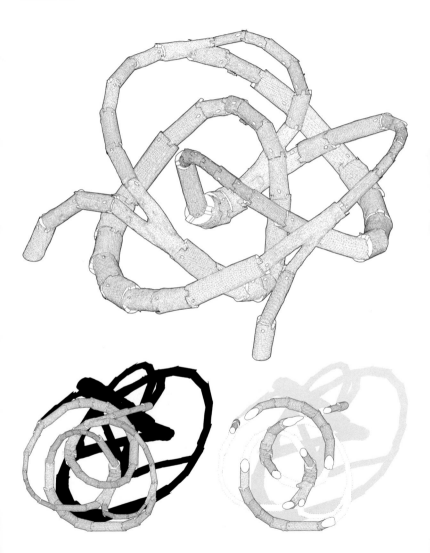

below: Detail view
of wood undulations

below center left:
Detail view of tree fork

bottom left: Detail view

bottom center: Detail
view of knot segment
at ground level

bottom right: Exploded
detail axonometric

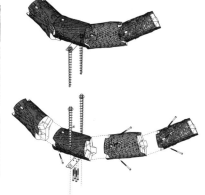

Leslie Lok and Sasa Zivkovic **93**

Open Source Factory

Ithaca, New York, 2017

Open-source frameworks have allowed widespread access to the technology and software for desktop-scale additive manufacturing, but at the large or industrial scale very few highly hackable open-source equipment platforms exist. The availability of such fabrication equipment, however, is critical as architectural research continues to employ robotic and digital technology to address large-scale experimentation and full-scale building construction.

Large-scale digital manufacturing equipment usually requires significant, often prohibitive start-up costs. Expanding on the Fab Lab and the RepRap, Open Source Factory takes advantage of the intradisciplinary expertise and interdisciplinary knowledge in construction machine design that has accumulated since the 2010s to democratize access to large-scale fabrication equipment.

The project incorporates two fabrication systems: Daedalus, a RepRap-based three-axis open-source CNC gantry, and Dionysus, a six-axis industrial robot system based on a decommissioned KUKA KR200/2. The machines offer radically different economic frameworks for implementing research in robotic fabrication into the academy, the research lab, design practice, or the small-scale building industry. Placing industrial robots and other large-scale fabrication tools within reach of all accelerates the sharing of research and the development of new ideas in building construction.

Project Team: Robotic Construction Laboratory (RCL), Cornell University; Christopher Battaglia, Reuben Chen, Todd Drucker, Peta Feng, Kieran Haruta, Brian Havener, Savannah Chasing Hawk, Yichen Jia, Yiyao Liu, Winnie Lu, Travis Nissen, Burak Unel, Chuqi Xiao, Mingyue Yang, Shiwoo Yu, Yang Zhao

below: Axonometric of robotic platform and safety cage

bottom left: Parts for Dionysus bandsaw end effector

bottom right: Dionysus cutting log with chainsaw end effector

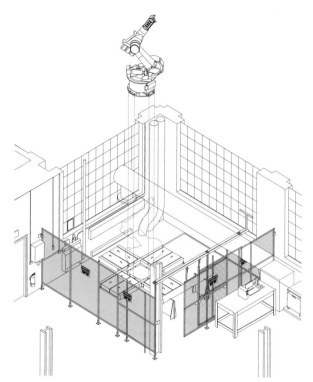

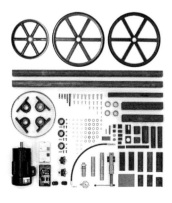

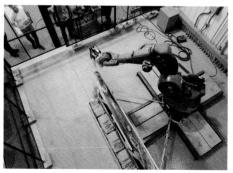

opposite top: Daedalus

opposite bottom:
Axonometric diagram
of Daedalus

below: Daedalus 3D
printing process

bottom: Daedalus parts

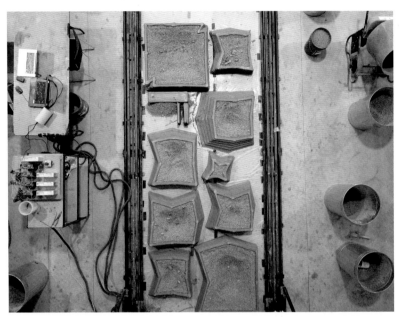

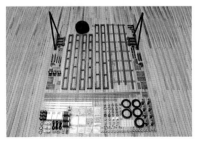

Isaac Michan Daniel

Michan Architecture

Given the context in which our work takes place, and the fact that our office sometimes takes on construction, we have no choice but to embrace uncertainty as part of the design process. A big part of what we do is address external contingencies. We try not to fight these factors but to accept them and even push them to their limits. We walk a fine line as we arrange and rearrange them with the goal of producing a cohesive body of work with an autonomous voice. Rather than seeing reality as something fixed, we question its systems and imagine new possibilities. We are never sure about what to expect from outside rules, or from within, and aim for the idea that the work should always surprise us.

We pursue architecture as a formal and material practice with a hands-on process. This process, which blends local craft with digital and analogue approaches, uses various media in a nonlinear sequence until the final stage of construction.

We try to respond with a provocation that produces its own set of questions. We strive to find a balance between the very familiar and the completely unexpected. At this midpoint the work speaks to our ancestors without copying them and simultaneously looks forward to new ways for matter and tectonics to misbehave.

Z53 Low-Cost Housing
Mexico City, Mexico, 2012

This residential complex, located in an area of Mexico City with high demand for affordable housing, interprets typical constraints—budget, materials, structure, and density—as opportunities. We modified traditional construction techniques to generate spatial qualities that respond to the local aesthetic, suggesting a new relationship between technology and tradition.

Three five-story structures, which contain a total of 42 units, are positioned to generate interior courtyards, which provide views and natural ventilation for each apartment. Two vertical cores and bridges above the patios connect the constituent portions.

The underground parking floor is structured with concrete columns; above, masonry brick walls carry the load. The masonry walls reinterpret traditional brick buildings, blurring the boundary between structure and ornament. We used a single red mud artisanal brick to produce varying yet cohesive facades that are sensitive to shadows and lights.

In collaboration with Grupo Nodus

opposite top: Facade

opposite bottom:
Facade detail
Photos: Rafael Gamo

below: Plan

opposite top left:
Vertical circulation

opposite top right:
View from a courtyard
Photos: Rafael Gamo

opposite bottom left:
Digital detail model of
brick facade

opposite bottom right:
Digital model of brick
pattern

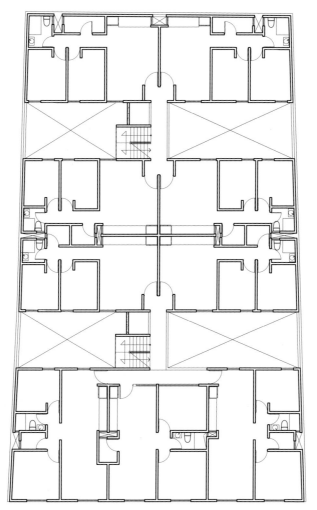

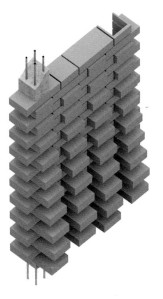

Pavilion ( )
Mextrópoli 2018
Mexico City, Mexico, 2018

The interior and exterior of Pavilion ( ) present an intriguing contradiction. Outside, the structure is a mute rectangular prism; inside, it reveals a completely different geometry: a void in the shape of an inverted vault. The negative space is a continuous surface without a roof: an oasis within the chaotic city center. Pavilion ( ) had a life span of just five days.

In collaboration with Colectivo Seis, Kababie Arquitectos, Taller Paralelo

Luma
Mexico City, Mexico, 2017

Luma Café, a small coffee shop in the Condesa neighborhood of Mexico City, occupies the ground floor of a commercial building.

The design "glitches" traditional materials—concrete, terrazzo, stucco, and felt—to generate interesting effects and textures. The tension between rough and polished finishes produces the character of the room.

The walls are finished in stucco, hatched by means of a traditional technique. The vertical raked lines disappear randomly, as if they were falling apart, on the lower parts of the walls. On the ceiling is a hanging "mega-lamp" consisting of a field of intersecting spheres. The "rocks" are made by hand-stitching pieces of felt cut with a CNC machine, creating a hybrid of digital and local craft. Suspended from the felt forms are cables with spotlights. These hanging components suggest a lower ceiling height, which results in a cozier space. The rock system and the cable system are intertwined, generating a controlled disorder in the café.

opposite: View toward coffee bar
Photo: Vicente Muñoz

below: Stucco wall hatches and felt "mega-lamp" with cables

opposite top right: Felt "mega-lamp" with cables against stucco wall

opposite top left: Detail of stucco hatches and concrete
Photos: Vicente Muñoz

opposite bottom: "Mega-lamp" rendering

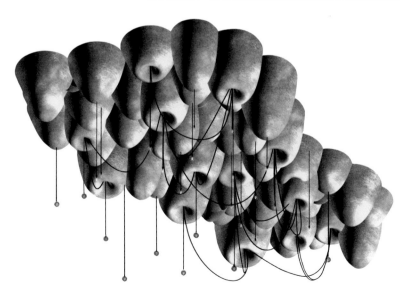

ODP Apartments

Mexico City, Mexico, 2018

The ODP residential complex is located in southwest Mexico City. The design follows the geometry of the L-shaped site, with two elongated components that produce a central garden, as well as its natural slope, which facilitates construction both above and below street level.

The project comprises 64 one-, two-, and three-bedroom units that are oriented to take advantage of light and views. Shared amenities include gardens, gym, multipurpose room, swimming pool, and, at the back of the site, a natural ravine.

The structure is partition walls with rigid frames and reinforced-concrete walls. Looking toward the street, the facade is exposed concrete with slender apertures that resemble scratches in the concrete. Looking inward, facades clad in vertical strips of travertine of varying widths produce a constant play of light and shadow.

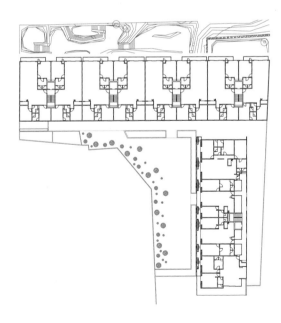

below: Side facade with vanishing apertures
Photo: Rafael Gamo

bottom left: View from balconies to internal garden
Photo: Rafael Gamo

bottom right: Travertine extrusions and cuts

opposite bottom: Concrete wall elevation

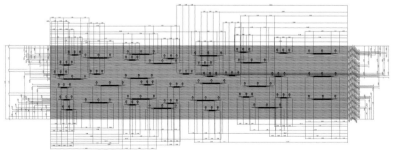

Oku
Mexico City, Mexico, 2018

The Japanese restaurant Oku is on the ground floor of an office building in northeast Mexico City. The kitchen and services occupy the back corner of the space, leaving the rest for reception, sushi bar, and interior and exterior seating.

A faceted concrete ceiling component, cut and shaped to adapt to program requirements, generates an interior space that is cohesive but still offers distinctive areas. Three "legs" descend from the ceiling, one that stretches to the floor to house the bathrooms, the other two accommodating light fixtures that frame the sushi bar. The inner surfaces of these components are clad in brass, which contrasts with the rawness of the concrete. Oak is used for the remainder of the interior.

opposite: Main dining area
Photo: Pepe Escárpita

below: Sushi bar
Photo: Yoshihiro Koitani

bottom left: Aluminum framing for ceiling component and "leg"

bottom right: Wood screen

opposite top: Concrete coating for ceiling component

opposite bottom: Worm's-eye view of ceiling component

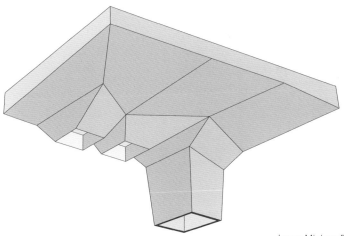

Desierto Apartments
Mexico City, Mexico, 2016

Desierto Apartments is a residential complex in southern Mexico City. The project is made up of 29 two- and three-bedroom units in a series of buildings staggered at the edge of the site. The arrangement adapts to the topography of the street and creates a large common garden at the center of the lot.

There is one apartment per floor in each structure. A vertical circulation core is posed between every two buildings. The public living spaces face the street over balconies in fair-faced concrete, which form the outer layer of the facade. Inclined columns connect the balconies from floor to floor. This composition both ensures privacy for the apartments and works as a structural element. Bedrooms and bathrooms receive light and air from the interior garden.

Our objective was to create spaces that are unique but also unified by means of shared language and materiality. In this way, the apartment complex values the identity of its residents.

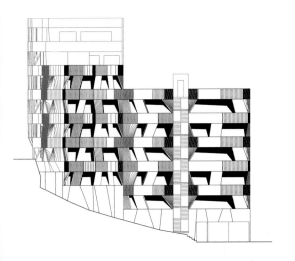

left: Elevation

opposite top:
Street view

opposite bottom:
Plan

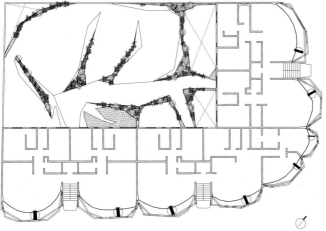

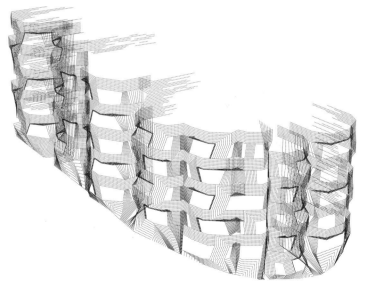

Ivi Diamantopoulou and Jaffer Kolb

New Affiliates

Sometimes we pause to look around and everything seems so full. Full of so many buildings, so many designs, so many designers, and so much stuff. So full that trash collecting and sorting are becoming increasingly paramount. So full that infrastructural management, hidden away for generations as an act of invisible labor, increasingly falls under public scrutiny and calls into question the value of newness. So full that we're ready to look back on ourselves and reassess what we make, and how we design.

We often think about value when we consider all this stuff in the context of our own practice. Working in New York, we confront high-end materials, consumer desire, gentrification, and waste—all formulations and expressions of value. Through these mechanisms, we see how value drives the market that drives architecture, and also a chance to shift the terms of valuation itself, to change how we practice. We sometimes think that what we value may say more about us than what we design.

So we've been looking at materials differently—at how they perform, where they come from, what they represent as cultural phenomena. We attempt to rewire the circuitry of how we consider use and how we construct desire. We want to assign value to forgotten things, historical things, discarded things. We say we are interested in reuse, but perhaps we are really interested in economic anthropology—in understanding systems of value through behavior, taste, and preference rather than efficiency. Culture counts! As do social relations, individual stories, and collective identities.

Our work ranges from public to intimate, open to private. Some of the questions we ask feel bigger than we are, but we approach them through the tools we cultivate as designers: space and form, materials and practice and flows, movement and systems of visuality. Even though we stay in our lane, we can't help rubbernecking. We borrow eclectically from any source, whether to scrounge for parts; to reconstruct fragments, surfaces, and forms from byproducts; or to find hidden moments of value. We invent new visual languages and disciplinary tools along the way. We are slowly becoming scavengers.

Test Beds

New York, New York, 2018–ongoing

This self-initiated research and design project, a collaboration with architectural historian Samuel Stewart-Halevy and the New York City Department of Parks and Recreation, looks to recycle architectural mock-ups as public infrastructure. Created as part of the design process and for testing at various scales, mock-ups represent investments of time and resources in the sequence of designing and building. The initiative engages this material resource and turns it into a building block for community infrastructure.

The size of mock-ups often corresponds to those of structures built in community gardens—casitas, sheds, greenhouses, shade structures—which prove to be ideal sites to relocate the fragments. Bringing the image of the growing city down to the ground allows the mock-ups to humanize the scale of the skyline and assign value to an overlooked resource. Ultimately they act as ambassadors, mining new possibilities from the world of development.

For the first of these projects, we are relocating a mock-up from a new condominium building—30 Warren Street in lower Manhattan—to the Garden by the Bay in Edgemere, Queens. We have used the developer-donated prototype, which models the cast-concrete facade system and window unit, as the dominant window wall in a new community facility. The structure comprises smaller buildings (shed, greenhouse, meeting room) under a shared roof, creating a collection of individually programmed spaces under a large shaded canopy, much needed in the beachside community.

Project team: Samuel Stewart-Halevy, Nashwah Ahmed, Audrey Haliman, Mike Babcock

opposite: Mock-up for new high-rise reused as greenhouse

opposite: Various mock-ups and garden structures

below: A piece of Tribeca as the cornerstone of community structure at Garden by the Bay, Edgemere, Queens

bottom: Mock-ups as urban bridges linking design, development, and neighborhood

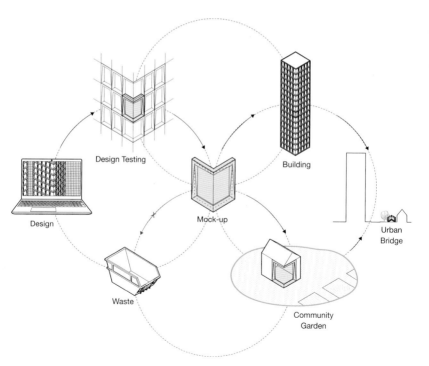

Design Testing

Building

Design

Mock-up

Urban Bridge

Waste

Community Garden

below: Pilot structure at Garden by the Bay

opposite top: Meeting room

opposite bottom left: Site plan

opposite bottom right: Greenhouse looking toward mock-up

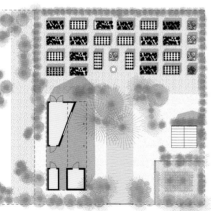

Museums Remuddled
New York, New York, 2019–ongoing

There is a kind of delirium in working with museums and galleries around New York. Exhibitions are temporary, going up and coming down as fast as even the most intrepid enthusiasts can remember to visit them. This situation means that the institutions that create the shows are hosts in constant flux: interiors assume a new identity with each display, surfaces are constantly hidden and revealed, and walls are relentlessly rearranged. And while the idea of architecture's elastic insides may be fascinating, the amount of waste produced is alarming.

We have teamed up with New York City's Department of Sanitation to understand how, while reworking the space of the museum, new design methods and new networks of material circulation can minimize refuse. This work leads to new details, atypical material choices, and the creation of invisible exchange networks.

For the exhibition *Leonard Cohen: A Crack in Everything* at New York's Jewish Museum, we worked with the Department of Sanitation to select as many materials as possible that could be repurposed, including custom-built displays, benches, surface finishes, dropped ceilings, and flooring. We specified materials that would resist wear (rubber flooring instead of carpet, benches with replaceable soft seating) and detailed them so as to minimize damage in removal. Ultimately, other than the drywall and studs, all surface materials, exhibition furniture, and temporary partitions were relocated after the exhibition.

Project Team: Audrey Haliman

opposite top: Imagining foam cladding across installations

opposite bottom: Bringing institutions together through waste

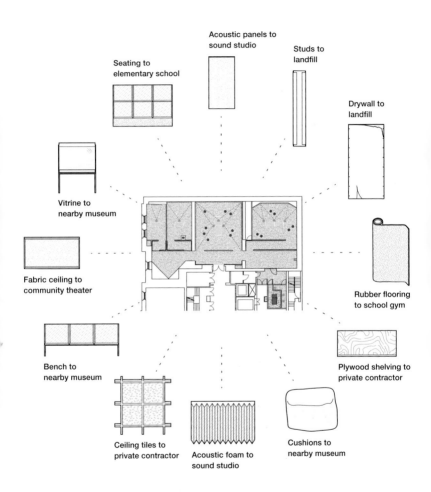

Acoustic panels to
sound studio

Studs to
landfill

Seating to
elementary school

Drywall to
landfill

Vitrine to
nearby museum

Fabric ceiling to
community theater

Rubber flooring
to school gym

Bench to
nearby museum

Plywood shelving to
private contractor

Ceiling tiles to
private contractor

Acoustic foam to
sound studio

Cushions to
nearby museum

top: Rubber flooring reused at playground   **bottom:** Vitrine reused at another museum

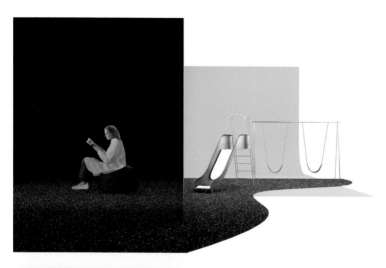

opposite: New kind
of temporary ornament
within the ornate halls
of the museum

below: Resilient
rubber flooring, easily
rolled for reuse
Photos: Michael Vahrenwald/Esto

Drywall is Forever
Performa Hub, Performa 19
New York, New York, 2019

As we look at our work with museums and galleries, we have been struck by drywall, both in its materiality and in what it represents in those spaces. Drywall is a temporary surface used to produce an image of apparent neutrality and permanence, even as it is constantly discarded and reinstalled. It piles up in dumpsters and contributes to the massive amount of waste produced by the construction industry.

Each year, 13 million tons of drywall are thrown away. Of that, 12 percent is "clean": unpainted and unused material scraps and contingency quantities. Recycling facilities, of which there are just a handful in the country, will process only clean scraps, leaving 88 percent as waste material that can become noxious under anaerobic conditions. And yet the art world tears down and rebuilds its own white walls as though the material was limitless and without consequences.

To find a design strategy that incorporates used material to produce a new type of gallery, we collected pieces of drywall from exhibitions being deinstalled around the city and used them to build a new gallery. This process created a kind of relief/decoration: puzzle pieces imprinting quietly on the surface itself. This new white cube records its own material make-up, rejecting that space's supposed neutrality and instead demonstrating the false perception that gypsum is seamless both in terms of its ecological footprint and its visible presence.

Project Team: Audrey Haliman

opposite top: New drywall assembly in progress

opposite bottom: White cube gallery marked by reclaimed drywall

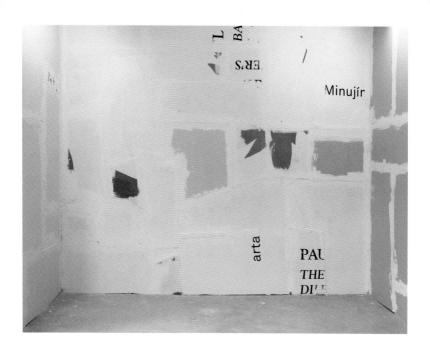

below: Detail view of new drywall assembly

bottom: Pile representing two days of "clean" drywall waste at USA Gypsum

opposite top: Construction and demolition waste in New York City (based on NEWMOA report, 2009)

opposite bottom: Conceptual elevation of drywall fragments assembled into new wall

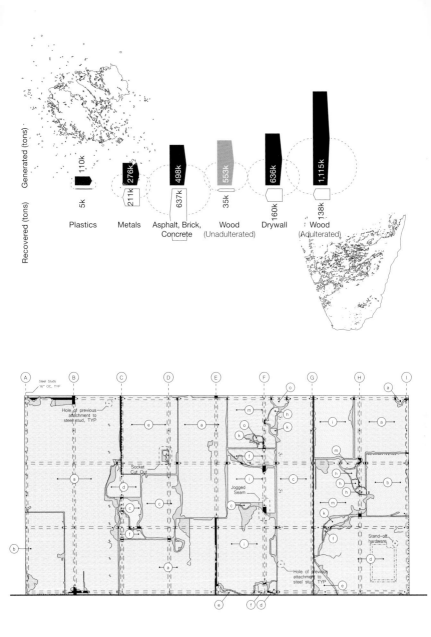

Generated (tons)

Recovered (tons)

110k	276k	498k	553k	636k	1,115k
5k	211k	637k	35k	160k	138k

Plastics   Metals   Asphalt, Brick, Concrete   Wood (Unadulterated)   Drywall   Wood (Adulterated)

Ivi Diamantopoulou and Jaffer Kolb **139**

01

Greene Naftali
Paul Chan
10.19.19

02

Brooklyn Museum
Titus Kaphar
10.13.19

03

MCNY
Cycling in the City
10.14.19

04

Clearing Gallery
Meriem Bennani
10.27.19

05

David Zwirner
Roy DeCarava
10.27.19

06

Gagosian Gallery
Zao Wou-Ki
10.26.19

07

Gavin Brown
Bethlehem Hospital
10.26.19

08

Gladstone Gallery
Walter Swennen
10.20.19

09

Hauser & Wirth
Eva Hesse
10.26.19

10

JTT
Elaine Cameron-Weir
10.27.19

11

Lévy Gorvy
Pierre Soulages
10.26.19

12

Matthew Marks
Vija Celmins
10.26.19

13

Wallach Art Gallery
After the End
10.6.19

14

The Morgan Library
Maurice Sendak
10.6.19

15

New Museum
Marta Minujín
10.29.19

16

Rubin Museum
Power of Intention
10.14.19

17

Wallach Art Gallery
After the End
10.6.19

18

Whitney Museum
Whitney Biennial
10.27.19

19

Luhring Augustine
Ritsue Mishima
10.26.19

20

Fergus McCaffrey
Ishiuchi Miyako
10.18.19

East New York Studios
Brooklyn, New York, 2019

Our conversion of a tea factory–turned–church into mixed-use art studios and galleries led to a revaluing of past material as well as careful documentation of how that material weaves its way through and around the newest life of the building. The building has been appended to many times since it was first constructed in the 1930s, leading to numerous idiosyncratic juxtapositions of materials, systems, and structures. We revealed the friction between these contrasts—found and new, rough and clean—through material assemblies inside and out. The new elements add to the layers of the building while altering, enlarging, and infilling some of the existing apertures. Our contribution attempts to rationalize the building while revealing its history.

Project Team: Ge Zhou, Tess Clancy
Architect of Record: Urban Design Workshop
MEP Engineer: ANZ Engineering
Structural Engineer: AST Engineering

below: Catalog
of found conditions
and new material

01 Studio VII

I-beam, overflow drain pipe,
1-hour partition

02 Studio II

2-hour partition, I-beam,
insulated pipe, joists

03 Foyer B

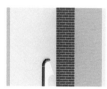

drywall, gooseneck pipe,
masonry wall

04 Studio VIII

1-hour partition, ceiling joist,
skylight framing, infill joist

05 Foyer A

masonry wall, insert window, drywall

06 Studio III

drywall partition, water pipe

07 Studio VII

drywall partition, water pipe

08 Common Area

masonry wall, drywall partition, I-beam

09 Hallway

masonry wall, steel post/beam/stair,
partial height partition, I-beam

10 Studio VI

2-hour drywall partition at 45°, joist

11 Hallway

masonry wall, crack infill

12 Studio V

drywall partition, joist, I-beam,
pipe, window

below: Studio with layout produced by found conditions

bottom left: Refurbished exterior with new brick infill

bottom center: Social and utility space behind entry gallery

bottom right: Infill window in previously dilapidated wall
Photos: Michael Vahrenwald/Esto

below: Drawing
of existing structure
incorporated into
new wall

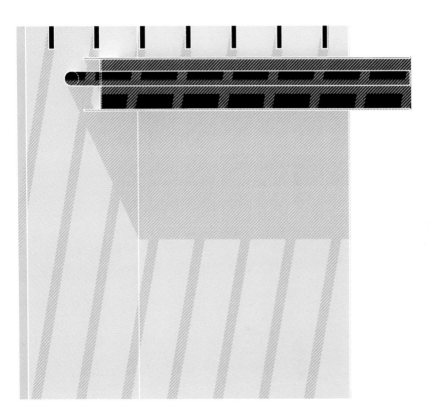

Farmstead Retreat
Three Oaks, Michigan, 2019

A growing tourism infrastructure along the eastern coast of Lake Michigan gave rise to this proposal to open up a working flower farm as an agritourism destination. The first phase consists of a 5,000-square-foot event venue; new visitor infrastructure; and new circulation paths that connect field to greenhouse and planting beds to scenic views. A second phase will include nine cabins based on a triangular module and using materials similar to those of the event space.

We began by looking to regional construction, especially steel barns and agricultural structures, which persuaded us to adopt a model of pre-engineered industrial architecture rather than one of hospitality design. By incorporating these materials and structural systems into the project, we found new value in an often-overlooked typology and material language both in a design vocabulary and in the building's economy and performance.

Project Team: Audrey Haliman

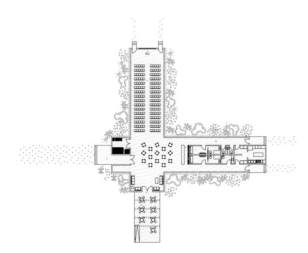

left: Plan

opposite top:
Pre-engineered
structure adapted for
program and site

opposite bottom:
Elevations

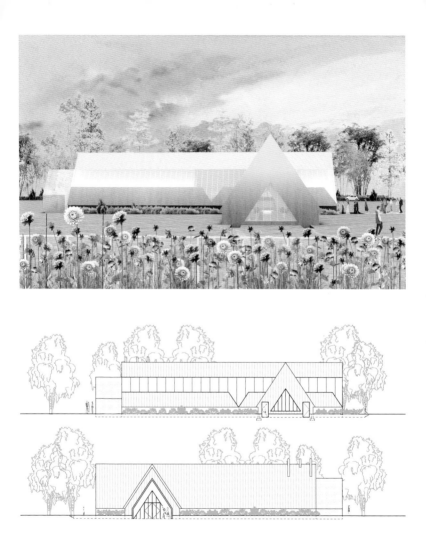

below: Highly textured
cabin interior

bottom: Drawings
of cabins showing
modular make-up

Elevation

Section A-A

Section B-B ◇ 1

Elevation

Section A-A

Section B-B ◇ 2

below: Three cabins
with different module
configurations

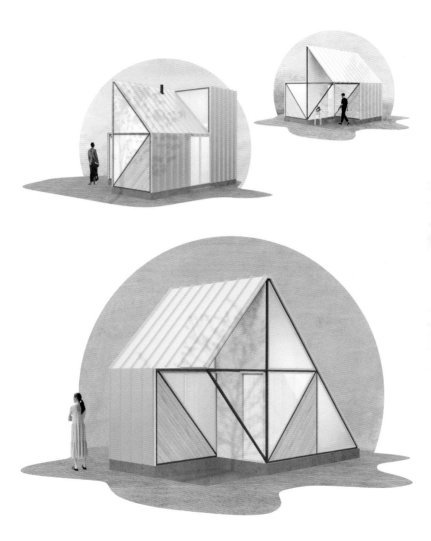

Luis Beltrán del Río García and Andrew Sosa Martínez

Vrtical

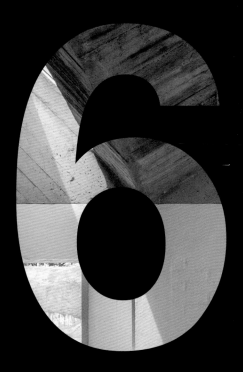

To value means to cherish. The habits and choices we cherish—joy, openness, diversity—define our work more than any finished space.

Our practice unfolds like a narrative. Incidents and anecdotes shape a project as much as constraints and materials, all piling up in our studio as the living matter of what we do. We find joy in every stage of this multipart process.

We are open to the unforeseen. While considerations of design are rooted in each project, so are whimsical and seemingly trivial but all-important details. We take great pleasure in how a client's memories, an abstruse drawing, or a chance conversation might shape a room or detail, creating atmosphere and becoming an abstraction of life. These intangibles are the most valuable part of our work. Every design is a new, distinct door to an open-ended transformation.

Diversity is a choice we have made. We founded Vrtical to satisfy a broad range of individuals and communities. In the tundra of Guanajuato is a temple conceived as a threshold. In Tlaxco is an artisans' market where local pine magnifies light. In Ocuilan de Arteaga is a house protected from the elements by endemic vegetation, among other means. In Mexico City is a sculptor's haven that secretes traces of the client's love for objects. Also in Mexico City is a modernist restoration, at once sensitive and liberal, that makes the building suitable for contemporary urban habitation.

Each project is different and tells its own tale. Yet each also illustrates the values we hold dear, the profession we cherish.

Threshold Temple
Cuerámaro, Mexico, 2017

Located ten kilometers outside the town of Cuerámaro, the Templo Umbral (Threshold Temple) is the first building commissioned by the Hare Krishnas since the group arrived in the region in 2012. It is intended to be the initial structure in a larger development.

The space, which can open completely on two sides, frames a view of the natural surroundings. Following the design criteria of Zen gardens, the walls, roof, and reflecting pool combine to set off the context.

The design strategy focused on understanding the principles of the Hare Krishnas, particularly their attitude toward collective engagement. An intuitive construction system that could be carried out by the community, who had virtually no training in building techniques, minimized labor costs. The temple bears a trace of the collaborative effort, allowing the participants to recognize their involvement.

left: Night view with open sides

opposite: East facade with reflecting pool

below left: Interior view **below right:** North facade with community-built brickwork **bottom:** Entrance

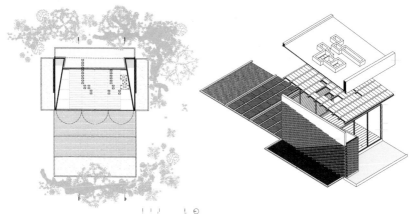

Luis Beltrán del Río García and Andrew Sosa Martínez **155**

Tlaxco Artisans Market

Tlaxco, Mexico, 2017

An urban development plan for Tlaxco, designated one of the country's "magical towns," was started with a market in an effort to boost the local economy and craft traditions. The building recovered the outer walls and foundations of a neglected older construction.

The market is organized into two main halls, a larger one with fourteen stalls for artisans from the district and a smaller one with workshops. The halls are connected to a courtyard. A walkway at the front, along the street, creates a dialogue between the contemporary and the vernacular by means of arches and a rectangular frame; the space is used as a meeting point.

The structural system consists of load-bearing walls and laminated pine roof trusses. Skylights along the length of the halls admit natural light while at the same time forming a prominent meeting point for the local population.

left: North facade

opposite: Main interior circulation

Photos: Rafael Gamo

bottom: Interior demolition of pre-existing market walls

below: Section

top: Axonometric

bottom: View from yard
Photos: Rafael Gamo

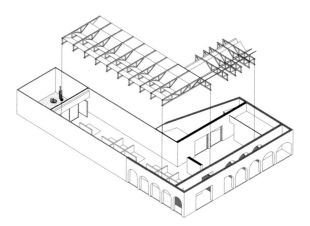

Luis Beltrán del Río García and Andrew Sosa Martínez **159**

below: View from
artisans' workshops

opposite: Semi-
public walkway
behind main facade
Photos: Rafael Gamo

Casa Valentina
Ocuilan de Arteaga, Mexico, 2018

Ocuilan de Arteaga, a town of 1,000 about 50 miles from Mexico City, lost many buildings to the Puebla earthquake of 2017. The reconstruction of numerous dwellings was sponsored by three organizations: Pienza Sostenible, Love Army, and Échale a Tu Casa.

The design of Casa Valentina was driven by two objectives. First, the client wanted to surround the house with her plants. Second, the limited budget suggested a building with an open shed roof supported by a lightweight steel truss structure. The inclined steel-deck roof shields the interior from both sun and rain. In the bedrooms, a second layer—a plywood ceiling mounted on wooden bars—provides protection from dirt and dust and maintains a relatively consistent interior temperature.

The house consists of three volumes with concrete-stabilized brick walls. Two outer components contain three bedrooms and semi-open living space. A smaller central module houses a bathroom. Next to the house is a small water tank atop a structure of pine posts.

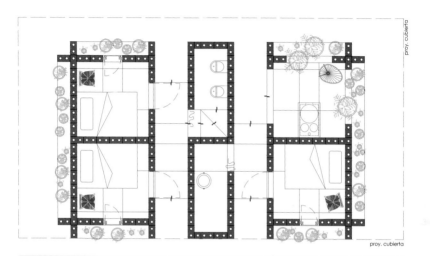

proy. cubierta

proy. cubierta

opposite: Corridor
between enclosed
volumes and semi-
open living room

below: Section

bottom left: Water
tank tower

bottom right: Brick-
work with structural
reinforcement

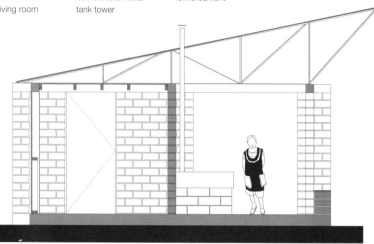

Pallares House and Studio

Mexico City, Mexico, 2020

The Pallares House and Studio, built for the sculptor Edna Pallares, provides both living space and art studio. The design was inspired by the materiality of the artist's work as well as a need for adequate light.

A corridor defined by walls in the shape of brackets connects all spaces. A concrete roof over the studio echoes the form of an industrial saw-tooth roof in a nod to brutalism. The structural system consists of brick and wooden beams. The module of the beams establishes a rhythm for architectural elements throughout the house. In some cases, the simple system acquires an ornamental complexity, as in the sculptural relief on the wall panels.

The client proposed alterations based on how she intended to inhabit the space. She also suggested embedding sculptures in the walls and floors to express her affection for these pieces.

opposite: Main
entrance leading
to art studio

below: Interior view
across patio
Photos: Rafael Gamo

below: Ground
floor plan

bottom: Roof terrace

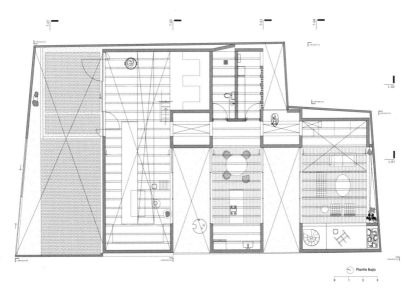

opposite: Main hallway   **below:** Living room
with home office
Photos: Rafael Gamo

Melchor Ocampo 38
Mexico City, Mexico, 2017

In 1940, Luis Barragán and Max Cetto designed a building known to historians as Four Painters' Studios. The structure deteriorated significantly over the decades and, by the time our client acquired it for use as an Airbnb, required a three-pronged approach to renovation.

First, we restored the original elements of the building using documentation from the Barragán Foundation in Switzerland and other sources. Second, we adapted the interior for vacation rentals—inserting kitchens, bathrooms, common laundry area, and guardhouse—under the assumption that increasing its habitability would facilitate its maintenance. Third, we reinterpreted some of the details characteristic of Barragán's mature works.

Post-renovation, the pale gray facade accentuates the unusual proportion of window to wall. Redesigned doors highlight the unexpected spatial sequences within the former studios. New stair skirtings match the original terrazzo plinths. Adjustments to the tiles are evidenced by brass joints. Street gates are similar to those in the Barragán House. These subtle details nod to a creator who was in the process of developing a mature language and also demonstrate the contemporary qualities of a forgotten but worthy building.

opposite: Evening view
Photo: Enrique Márquez Abella

Luis Beltrán del Río García and Andrew Sosa Martínez **173**

below left: Building before renovation

below right: Elevation of renovated facade

bottom left: First and third floor plans

bottom right: Second and fourth floor plans

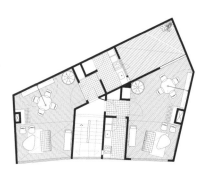

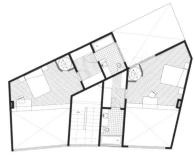

Left, top to bottom:
Julian Rose and
Garrett Ricciardi, Sasa
Zivkovic and Leslie Lok,
David Eskenazi

**Right, top to
bottom:** Isaac Michan
Daniel, Jaffer Kolb and
Ivi Diamantopoulou,
Andrew Sosa Martínez
and Luis Beltrán del
Río García